FATAL SUNSET:
VANISHED BEAUTY

MARK YOSHIMOTO NEMCOFF

Glenneyre Press

Los Angeles, CA

ISBN: 1-934602-31-0
ISBN-13: 978-1-934602-31-7

Published by Glenneyre Press, LLC.
Los Angeles, CA
www.wordsushi.com

First Edition

Cover design by: MYN

VANISHED BEAUTY is dedicated to the memories of Robyn Gardner and Tina Watson.

I am not telling you to avoid going on vacation.
This book only asks one thing:

DARE TO BE AWARE!

≈ *1* ≈

The spirited beauty stares back at me from the photograph. She's on a beach somewhere, relaxed and happy; my eyes keep dancing over her playful smile and those gleaming pearly whites. Her golden hair is barely restrained by a dark pair of sunglasses. A recently plucked orchid, the color of a ripe magenta mulberry, is tucked behind her ear. Her shoulders are tanned and toned, a marked contrast to the visible string of her black bikini top.

Time and again my gaze returns to her effusive smile, as large as life. Larger.

Her smile is alive. Her eyes are alive.

The face that looks back at me from this photo wants to tell me something.

The smile is not born of abandon or whimsy, caught with the subject candid and unaware. No, this smile is intended for the camera, posed, a deliberate memory registered through the lens.

There's no doubt the smile is genuine. It's not worn like a mask to hide pain; there is nothing forced about it.

It is a happy smile, honest and intentional.

It is the grin of someone who, for this sliver of captured time, feels carefree and liberated from the burdens of life. It's a vacation smile.

It belongs to Robyn Colson Gardner and I can't stop staring at it. Her face utterly haunts me.

This is the same Robyn Colson from Mount Airy, Maryland, a suburb of Washington D.C. that managed to retain its small town charm and appeal despite nearly two centuries. It is the same Robyn Colson who finally grew up to become a class of '94 graduate from South Carroll High School in the nearby town of Skyesville.

It is the same Robyn Colson who once married to became Robyn Gardner and who, seventeen years later, vanished without a trace from Aruba, on August 2, 2011 — almost exactly like Natalee Holloway did in 2005.

The parallels between the cases of Holloway, the 18 year-old recent high school graduate, and Gardner, the 35 year-old outgoing and vivacious aspiring model, are jaw-dropping to say the least. Both blonde and pretty. Both about the same build: 5'4"-5' 5" tall and weighing 110 pounds.

Both stayed in the same Aruban resort town of Oranjestad.

Just like Natalee Holloway, Robyn Gardner was rumored to have been buried alive in the Aruban sand.

However, there is a big difference between the two cases. The last person to allegedly see Natalee Holloway alive, 25 year old Joran van der Sloot, sits rotting in a Peru jail after confessing to murdering and robbing a young woman named Stephany Flores. Ironically, that crime took place on the fifth anniversary of Holloway's disappearance.

The last person to allegedly see Robyn Gardner alive still walks free on his own recognizance. Gary Giordano, the 50 year old CEO of Gaithersberg Maryland IT and staffing company Leverage LLC, who was Robyn Gardner's unlikely final traveling companion, continues to maintain his innocence. That innocence has been called into question several times by Robyn's family; because of the odd circumstances surrounding Robyn's story and the lurid details that would eventually come to light, it isn't hard to see why.

It all started with a lie.

Richard Forester, Robyn's 40 year old boyfriend, believed he knew her well. Robyn was supposedly on vacation in Orlando, Florida with her parents. However, listening to her phone call from his Frederick, Maryland apartment, something sounded quite odd to Forester. There were noises and beeping on the phone line; the call sound like it was coming from somewhere out of the United States.

Robyn said she couldn't talk. The next morning, a message from her popped up in Forester's email inbox. It said her parents had surprised her with a family trip to Aruba.

That was Monday, August 1, 2011.

Just past 2 a.m. the next day, Robyn visited Forester's Facebook page. "This sucks," she posted on his wall. The odd message, posted from her iPad, raised Forester's concern.

"Inbox me," he replied, concerned.

When she didn't respond, ten hours later he desperately posted, "Where r u baby??"

Sometime around 3 p.m. on Tuesday, a message from Robyn appeared in Forester's inbox. "I love you, I care about you and we'll talk about this and sort it out when we get back." Her words echoed a strain in their relationship that neither could ignore.

It would be the last Richard Forester would ever hear from her.

≈ 2 ≈

Wednesday and Thursday, Forester's Gmail chat window showed that Robyn was online. However, there was still no contact from her. The green indicator next to her name made it look like her account was actively signed in.

He messaged: "Hello. I know you're online. Tell me what you're pissed about."

He received no response.

Throughout the day Forester would email Robyn. "Is this how you're trying to break up with me?" The lovelorn boyfriend urgently tried to reach her for any answer and got none.

Robyn was scheduled to return home from her trip Thursday night. At the very least, Forester thought they would sort it out then. She failed to return, and Forester's anxiety grew into panic.

It got worse. Friday morning Andrew Colson, Robyn's brother, delivered terrible news. Robyn's mother had received a call the day before: Robyn was presumed missing at sea.

"How could that be?" thought Richard.

This was only the first of many shocks to come. As it turned out, *no one in Robyn Gardner's family even knew she was in Aruba.* It was not a surprise family trip at all.

Robyn was a spirited girl; it was not surprisingly for her to occasionally take off on the odd spontaneous trip. Even so, what her family and boyfriend learned next fell beyond the scope of "spontaneous."

Robyn hadn't gone to Aruba alone. Her traveling companion was Gary Giordano, a 50 year-old man whose name was familiar to Forester. Giordano was one of Robyn's online friends, a platonic buddy — who wore what appeared to be a badly mismatched toupee — that Robyn had even gone so far as to describe as her "gay friend."

The circumstances of the Aruba trip, along with Robyn's concealment of the truth, now threw everything she had previously said about Giordano into question — especially now that she was missing.

According to Giordano, that Wednesday he and Robyn had gone to a beach on Aruba's southern tip for some early evening snorkeling. Everything went fine until he realized they were being pulled out to sea by the strong tide. He tapped on Robyn's leg to signal that they should head back in.

After fighting the current back to the shallows, Giordano alleged that he turned, exhausted from the challenging swim, expecting Robyn to be right behind him. She was nowhere to be found.

The time: roughly 6 p.m. — just three hours after Robyn's last message to Forester.

Giordano claimed he immediately phoned police, very concerned that Robyn had somehow been swept out to sea by the strong current. Authorities began searching the shore and surrounding area around the resort town of Orajestad. Even as Richard Forester was hearing about this for the first time — 36 hours later — police helicopters and Coast Guard boats continued to scour the coastline for any sign of yet another beautiful blonde American tourist who had vanished from an Aruban beach without a trace.

That morning, while members of Robyn's family tried to remain calm and cling to the hope that she would be found safe somewhere else on the island, her mother flew to Aruba to personally search for her missing daughter. After meeting with authorities there, she was introduced to Giordano, a literal stranger to her who had been identified as the last man to see Robyn alive.

Andrew Colson would later describe his mother's perception of Gary Giordano as calm, perhaps too calm, without a hint of sorrow.

Richard Forester grew more and more suspicious of Giordano's story. Having been with Robyn for two years, he was doubtful that she would willingly go out snorkeling at all.

"We went on vacations and I couldn't even get her to put her head under water in the pool. She was into makeup and hair, and knowing her, she would have had a few cocktails already and would only be getting ready to go out that night," Forester would eagerly tell the reporters who were quickly lining up to get his side of this tragic story.

Apparently, Forester wasn't the only one who found the Maryland businessman suspicious. That Friday, hours after meeting with Robyn's mother, Giordano passed through security and U.S. Customs at Aruba's airport. He explained to officials that he was changing flights because of weather, adding that his traveling companion was "taking another flight." Mere feet from leaving Aruba, Giordano was arrested as he tried to board his plane. Authorities noticed something quite obvious: Giordano was drenched in sweat.

≈ *3* ≈

Strange behavior alone is not a surefire indicator of guilt. However, authorities in Aruba were skeptical enough to keep the nervous 50 year-old Gary Giordano locked up while they took a closer look at what was now a potential murder. What the investigation into the aspiring model's disappearance uncovered would completely redefine the image of Gary Giordano in the eyes of the world.

Back home, Forester faced the media. He revealed to one online gossip outlet that he and Robyn had discussed marriage. "She had her own apartment in Frederick, but she lived with me six days a week," he stoically told the reporter. "She had her cats here." He added that they were actually in the process of looking for a place together.

Forester also became sadly aware of nasty rumors concerning the exact nature of Robyn's relationship with this other man. Robyn had clearly met Giordano online over a year before her disappearance. Initially, it was reported the two had connected through Match.com, the same site where she had met Forester. That Robyn was still frequenting Internet dating sites was news to her boyfriend.

"It's not important to me right now," he emphatically stated when questioned about the circumstances of Robyn's trip. "That's for her and I to discuss when she comes back." He continued to speak of her in the present tense, hopeful for his girlfriend's safe return. "I don't know when she would have time to see anyone else."

Back in Aruba, the hot water Gary Giordano found himself in hadn't cooled one bit. Authorities were beginning to question certain aspects of his story. He claimed that, fearing for his life snorkeling in the rough water, he signaled for Gardner to go to shore. Yet, as he kicked against the strong current, not once did he turn to check if she had followed. "I only looked back when I hit a rock," Giordano told investigators. "Before that I did not look back. I was only busy saving my life."

The police also noticed scrapes on their suspect's legs. When asked how he had gotten them, Giordano answered that he didn't know.

Upon searching the public beach behind the Rum Reef Bar & Grill, investigators had discovered a bloody palm print and an unused condom straight out of the package. If either of these pieces of supposed evidence factored into Robyn's disappearance, Giordano wasn't talking. In fact, he wasn't saying much at all.

Then a new witness came forth, disputing Giordano's account of the events of August 2. Local fisherman Sergio Silva was casting for bonefish and snapper off Baby Beach. There, he allegedly spotted Robyn and Giordano walking along the reef around 4 p.m. According to Silva, the couple never went into the water. Instead, they got into a car, drove away, and did not return.

That would not even be the most disturbing detail to emerge that week. Things in the Robyn Gardner case were about to take a darker, much seedier turn.

Under interrogation by authorities, Giordano revealed that he had purchased an American Express travel insurance policy for Robyn Gardner that named himself as the beneficiary. In the event of an accidental death, that policy was worth a cool $1.5 million.

As the Associated Press reported, within two days of reporting Robyn missing, Giordano attempted to collect on that insurance money.

"We are investigating that material to see if it bears any relevance to the investigation," Aruba's chief prosecutor, Solicitor General Taco (yes, "Taco") Stein told reporters just five days after Giordano's arrest.

Former FBI special agent Brad Garrett suggested to one major American news network that the insurance policy definitely raised further questions about Giordano's intentions.

"Was this premeditated? Had he planned all along to lure her to Aruba and kill her for the insurance money? It has that flavor to it, but we'll

MARK YOSHIMOTO NEMCOFF

have to see how evidence bears out," Garrett said. "It becomes extremely important when you add all the other pieces to what we know about Mr. Giordano. By adding this piece it obviously takes on a completely different context than preventative insurance of two people."

At least in the court of public opinion, the existence of such a policy offered up a potential motive in the case. To some, FBI Agent Garrett's words eerily echoed the story of Tina Watson.

≈ *4* ≈

Christina Mae "Tina" Thomas was born on February 13, 1977. In October of 2003, at the age of 26, Tina would marry David Gabriel "Gabe" Watson and die just eleven days later during her honeymoon in Australia.

Gabe and Tina met at the University of Alabama at Birmingham while sharing classes together. Gabe tried unsuccessfully in getting a date with Tina; all attempts to ask her out resulted in him being shot down.

It wasn't until a party on New Years Eve 2001 that things between the pair began to click. Sometime before Christmas, Gabe purchased a certain handbag for Tina while in New York City. A few weeks after the party, Gabe and Tina were officially a couple.

Though it seemed to some that Gabe wasn't able to commit to a permanent relationship with Tina, in mid-February of 2003 Gabe asked Tina's father,

Tommy Thomas, for permission to marry his daughter. When it came time to pop the question to Tina on Easter Sunday 2003, Gabe typed up a note with the proposal and hid it in her apartment. Tina Thomas had always loved Easter egg hunts, and this one had a reward better than chocolate.

Gabe planned the scuba trip months in advance. Just off Cape Bowling Green, Queensland, in the central section of the Great Barrier Reef Marine Park, lay the wreck of the *SS Yongala* — a 350 foot long passenger ship hit by a cyclone in 1911 before taking all 122 souls aboard to the ocean floor.

The *Yongola* had been on a routine trip from Melbourne to Townsville, its 99th in the eight years since it had been christened by the Adelaide Steamship Company to run the busy and profitable route linking the gold fields of Western Australia. A champagne celebration had been planned for the *Yongala*'s 100th voyage from Cairns back to Melbourne the following week.

On March 23, 1911, the lighthouse keeper on nearby Dent Island could see the *Yongala* on the horizon just as word came via the newly installed Australian wireless service that a cyclone was headed their way. Though desperate to warn the ship of the massive storm brewing in her path, the lighthouse keeper was unable to radio the *Yongala*; the wireless radio it was supposed to carry onboard was still en route from the Marconi Company in England.

It was not until the *Yongala* failed to show up at the port of Townsville that anyone suspected trouble. A fleet of rescue boats went searching for her, to no avail. Only after wreckage and cargo from the *Yongala* washed ashore at Cape Bowling Green was it certain that the *Yongala* and all those aboard had been lost.

Rediscovered in 1958, the ghostly wreck of the *Yongala* lay in approximately 30 meters of water, with its upper section just 16 meters below the water's surface. Referred to by some as the Australian *Titanic,* time had transformed the *Yongala* into an artificial reef, making it a complex and thriving habitat for sea life as well as a very popular destination for divers.

Gabe already had scuba experience. Along with his close childhood friend Mike Moore, Gabe took a diving course in 1996. Beginning in a swimming pool, then advancing to a fenced-in pool in the icy waters of a sunken quarry known as Alabama Blue Water Adventures, and then finally the controlled environment of Morrison Springs in Florida, Gabe Watson completed his diving course. At this point, Gabe was hooked. He gained his open water certificate in May 1998, an advanced open water certificate in August 1998, and a rescue dive certificate in April 1999.

In July of that year, he and Mike went on a dive trip to Cozumel, Mexico. One day, while swimming 50 feet down, a dive weight fell out of Mike's buoyancy compensator device (BCD). The BCD is an air vest that helps the diver rise or sink. The push of one button inflates the BCD; another button lets air out so the diver can descend. Without the additional dive weight, Mike began floating to the surface. Despite having problems with his ears, Gabe dove down 75 feet to retrieve the weight for his buddy.

By the time of the wedding, Gabe had completed 55 dives, including six at night. In the twelve months prior, he had completed a dozen dives, the deepest being 150 feet.

Tina, on the other hand, was completely green behind the gills when it came to scuba. As Gabe was consumed by his favorite hobby, it was clear to Tina that if she wanted to see him on the weekends she would have to take up diving too. Gabe talked her into taking a dive course.

The scuba trip to The Great Barrier Reef had been promised as a graduation present from Gabe's parents and grandmother. It was Tina's idea to transform it into their dream honeymoon. She timed it in order to catch the annual sea turtle migration so they could see actual clown fish like a real life "Nemo."

On March 7, 2003, Tina began her first instructional dives in a swimming pool, then later at the same Birmingham quarry where Gabe learned how to scuba. She finished her course on June 8, just two months before the wedding. Finally, everything was set for the dream honeymoon of a lifetime.

If Tina had always wanted to be a princess, she certainly looked the part on Sunday October 11, 2003 as she walked down the aisle of the Southside Baptist Church in Birmingham, clad in a lovely white gown, face beaming.

Gabe did everything he could not to tear up when he first laid eyes on his beautiful bride. After Gabe and Tina had been pronounced man and wife, video footage captured the joyous moment when the two went back down the aisle hand-in-hand, almost skipping.

The couple arrived in Sydney, Australia on October 15. They spent nearly a week taking in sights such as Darling Harbor, the Sydney Opera House, Taronga Zoo and the National Maritime Museum. From there, Gabe and Tina travelled to Townsville.

As planned, the first half of the honeymoon would be Tina's week; the second half, Gabe's. Before leaving the United States, Gabe had booked a seven night scuba cruise with Mike Ball Dive Expedition aboard the luxury dive boat *Spoilsport*.

Around 8 pm on October 21, Gabe and Tina boarded the *Spoilsport* with nearly two dozen other passengers and three commercial divers. With the exception of air tanks and weights, which were to be provided by the boat, the Watsons had brought all of their own dive gear from home. Leaving port after 11:30, the *Spoilsport* embarked to their first dive spot, 48 nautical miles southeast from Townsville and 12 nautical miles east of Cape Bowling Green.

Assessing the diving qualifications of those aboard was the responsibility of the trip's divemaster, Wade Singleton. He suggested to the Watsons that Tina undertake a daytime orientation dive with a professionally trained driver. Tina declined, saying she was comfortable diving with

Gabe as her trusted dive buddy to assist in case of difficulty.

Following breakfast onboard and a briefing by the dive crew between 9am and 9:30am, divemaster Singleton again suggested that Tina take a training dive. Once more, she made it clear she felt safe with Gabe.

Gabe and Tina readied to hit the water, each donning a wetsuit, mask, fins, BCD and air tank. It was a beautiful day and the red flag was out.

Divers wear a computer to time the speed of the diver's ascent to avoid surfacing from deep water too quickly; this can create a deadly condition known as decompression sickness, commonly known as "the bends." The dive computer also tracks of the depth of a dive and the duration spent underwater. Each device was made up of two parts, a sensor attached to the outside of the wetsuit and a wrist-worn indicator that displayed all important data like a giant digital watch. The Watsons had each brought their own personal dive computers from home.

Once Gabe and Tina geared up, they boarded a motorized dinghy. It was a short ride with four other divers to the access point on the *Yongala*'s bow. Here, they entered the water.

Right away, Gabe began signaling that there was a problem with his dive computer. He returned to the *Spoilsport* with Tina in tow so that he could reposition the device's batteries. Once done, the couple re-entered the water.

Six minutes into their second attempt to dive, Tina lost consciousness and sank to the bottom, 90 feet below the water's surface.

Shortly before the Watsons had married, Gabe had asked Tina to increase her life insurance policy and to make him beneficiary.

≈ *5* ≈

The $1.5 million policy Gary Giordano had taken out on Robyn Gardner was not exactly a smoking gun, and investigators and observers knew it.

"The key with this case, assuming you don't find Robyn Gardner, is that you're going to have to put together a very strong circumstantial case — that it was premeditated, that he (Giordano) used a ruse to get here there," stated former FBI special agent Brad Garrett .

To boyfriend Richard Forester, these new revelations about the insurance policy were quite disturbing. "I can't believe Robyn would ever sign something like that voluntarily. Maybe if she was forced to, maybe if she was misinformed to what it was," he said.

Though Forester continued to hold out hope of seeing Robyn alive again, Aruban authorities had already lost faith in her safe return. The island-wide search for Robyn was halted. Taco Stein echoed the pessimism: "With all the publicity in the case, if she were alive she would have made herself known."

By this time, even though he had not officially been charged with anything, Giordano was reportedly refusing to cooperate with investigators.

Police began to retrace the pair's last steps together. After discovering Giordano and Robyn had dined at the Rum Reef Bar & Grill at Baby Beach on August 2, just hours before she went missing, police talked to restaurants staff members who claimed that Giordano's blonde companion seemed woozy.

Giordano explained that the couple had been drinking vodka back at the Marriott before arriving for their late lunch. According to sources, he also mentioned that Robyn had taken sleeping pills earlier in the day.

Surveillance video confirmed that the two had been there. It also showed Giordano parking a rental Toyota Rav-4 mini SUV behind the bar, not once but twice. Giordano explained he moved after he decided to park in the shade. Because of the Rav-4's tinted windows, authorities couldn't confirm the identities of anyone else inside the car.

Another thing was becoming clear to investigators: Giordano was frequently difficult to identify in the surveillance videos they obtained because he allegedly changed toupees on a frequent basis.

The details of the timeline for August 2 were slowly coming into focus. Seen on surveillance video at approximately 6:02 p.m., a few hours after dining there and only minutes after he claimed he realized that Robyn had not made it back to shore, Giordano tapped on the closed shutters of the Rum Reef Bar to get the attention of anyone inside.

But in what some may categorize as a lack of urgency, it was almost twenty minutes later before Giordano headed to the back kitchen of the bar to tell someone to call the police.

It was this troubling and quickly-expanding pool of circumstantial evidence, along with word of blood found on a rock behind the dive shop at the Rum Reef Bar & Grill, which was painting Gary Giordano in a decidedly negative light. There were additional reports that, less than a half hour after calling police, Giordano excused himself to go back to his hotel room so he could nap. Circumstantial or not, that was enough to convince Judge Monique Yarzagaray to rule that Giordano be held for additional interrogation.

That wouldn't be all. Complicating matters even further, more disturbing and shocking details quickly emerged about Aruba's prime suspect.

≈ 6 ≈

Blonde, beautiful, and now missing, Robyn Gardner took a secret trip to Aruba that no one in her family knew about until two days after she vanished. Because of the striking similarities to the mysterious disappearance of American teenager Natalie Holloway, from the exact same Aruban town just six years earlier, eager media outlets all over the world swarmed the area to find the newest morsels of this juicy story.

Robyn had been married before. In 1998, she wed a six-foot, eight inch tall construction executive named Kenneth Gardner. The couple had lived well in Frederick, another tiny Washington D.C. Suburb. Their life together was the American Dream, complete with a Mercedes Benz in the driveway and a pair of mortgages on their house.

Kenneth had been a division president at Dan Ryan Builders, a massive construction company specializing in the development of communities of single-family houses, townhomes and duplexes throughout Maryland, Pennsylvania, Virginia, West Virginia, and North Carolina. Like many Americans, Ken lost his job when the economy turned sour. He tried to launch his own construction company, The Gardner Building Group. However, things hadn't worked out so great.

Robyn and Kenneth separated in 2007 and subsequently divorced in May of 2009. What few knew at the time of her disappearance was that the former couple was locked in a battle over alimony. Upon their separation, Kenneth Gardner had been ordered to make two lump sum payments to Robyn totaling $30,000, plus pay her $2,000 every month for three years. Kenneth had petitioned the court to modify the amount and now Robyn was fighting against it.

According to Forester's timeline, he and Robyn had been together for two and a half years, meaning they would have met during her separation from Kenneth. If Robyn had any other boyfriends, Forester certainly didn't know about them. The nature of the relationship between her and the much older Gary Giordano was growing murkier with each passing revelation.

"His past worries me," Forester said when asked about Giordano, "I have had a few people who have dated him in the past reach out to me. They say he is aggressive and angry."

Back in Aruba, Giordano's lawyer, Michael Lopez, was busy pushing back against the highly-negative aspersions being cast upon his client.

Lopez claimed that Giordano had cooperated fully with authorities and should be immediately released due to lack of evidence against him.

Proof or not, the mention of Giordano's name brought plenty of interesting folks out of the woodwork; each had stories to tell about the suspicious Maryland businessman now spending 17 hours a day being questioned by authorities inside of a sweltering 9x9 Aruban jail cell.

Gary Giordano lived in a $1.3 million stone mansion in the upper class D.C. suburb of Gaithersburg, which he allegedly used — along with his charm, bluish-green eyes and many promises — to court women. The things revealed about him would soon lead some to wonder if Giordano harbored a dangerous personality.

Sharon Cohen was in a position to know Gary Giordano quite well. The pair wed in 1987 and she was mother to his three boys — a 19 year-old and 14 year old twins. However, by 2001, the marriage had deeply hit the skids. In light of Robyn's disappearance, what Cohen wrote in court papers about her soon-to-be ex was chilling.

"He can't control his anger."

Giordano would also point the finger back at Cohen, alleging that during a heated argument she struck him with a cooking spoon. Cohen countered with claims of physical displays of Giordano's ongoing nasty temper — accusations that would include destroying a computer, throwing phones and violently shoving one of their sons to the ground.

On December 10, 2001, a domestic violence case against Gary Giordano was filed in the Circuit Court of Montgomery County, Maryland naming

Cohen as the defendant. Court records revealed a petition for protection from her husband. Eleven days later, she would file for divorce.

That divorce from Cohen in April of 2003 would be Giordano's first. In 2006, he would wed someone new only to have that marriage suffer the same ending just two years later in 2008.

Soon after, a curious pattern would emerge. Other women Giordano became involved with all fit a very similar physical profile to Robyn Gardener: thin and blonde. If his dating history was any indication, Giordano had developed a "type."

Jeanette Farago, an ex-neighbor of Giordano's, started to date him around the time of his second divorce. Initially, Farago thought the suave businessman to be "Mr. Perfect." Her suburban dream soon turned into a nightmare as Giordano became possessive and prone to stalking. It was not uncommon for him to spy on Farago; detailed text messages describing her current outfit would pop up on her cell phone — his way of letting her know he was watching. If she told him she was going to the market, Giordano demanded photographic evidence as proof.

Giordano was also prone to electronic snooping. He insisted that she divulge her email password so he could check to make sure she wasn't sneaking around behind his back.

Even more curious, Farago revealed that Giordano had offered to take her on a two-week cruise and even went so far as to buy her a ticket. When she refused to go, he became irate. On another occasion, Giordano hid in the woods behind her house, wearing a deer mask. He then popped up outside her window, illuminating his strange visage with a cigarette lighter.

"He was really creepy and scary," she told reporters. "He scared the bejesus out of me."

Was this a case of Giordano presenting himself as the charismatic Dr. Jekyll only to eventually morph into the violent Mr. Hyde?

In the summer of 2009, Giordano met another woman on the Internet. Later, to her great shock and surprise, she discovered that he had clandestinely filmed them having sex. Even more disturbing was how the discovery was made: he had posted images of her on the web — the kind most people would never expect to see of themselves unless they were porn stars.

After she confronted him, Giordano purportedly printed up indecent photos of her and stuffed them into the mailboxes of several of her neighbors.

She filed abuse allegations against him on February 4, 2010. In court papers, she swore he once told her that "the world would be a better place without" her.

He also added that "he could help."

The woman's attorney, Gail Landau, would paint an even darker picture of her client's alleged abuser. "She was scared to death of the man. She thought he was capable of great anger and violence."

Though the woman would eventually be granted a restraining order against ex-lover Gary Giordano, in the end no criminal charges were ever filed by

Montgomery County prosecutors. Even though State's Attorney John McCarthy's office met with Landau's client several times, she ultimately chose not to pursue charges.

Her client's desire to drop the case, according to Landau, was due to fear.

Steven Kupferberg, a lawyer for Gary Giordano, tells it differently, "I suspect there wasn't anything to the allegations in terms of illegality." He deemed the story of the secret sex video to be "likely exaggerated."

Kupferberg added his client had been wronged, too. Giordano alleged he was slandered based upon letters and e-mails he claimed she had sent to others.

Back in Aruba, Solicitor General Taco Stein debunked the theory that a pink shirt and black sandals found during the search of an abandoned phosphate mine in Oranjestad belonged to Robyn Gardener. Also, it was confirmed by investigators that Giordano did indeed have snorkeling equipment at the time of the incident.

Still, given how obsessive Robyn was about the fastidious appearance of her hair and makeup, the very idea that she would go snorkeling in the first place rang very false with Richard Forester. Because Robyn's family was refusing to talk to the media, he took on the burden of being the public voice for those who loved Robyn most. He continued to hammer at Giordano's character.

"I've had people come out from his past who have contacted me and told me some pretty bad details, so I definitely have a very bad feeling,"

Forester told the *Today Show*'s Matt Lauer. "I just try to stay optimistic and hopeful that she'll be back and returned safely."

However, without Robyn's body, all Aruban authorities had against Giordano was circumstantial. At their behest, the FBI gathered some agents from their Maryland field office and raided Gary Giordano's home in Gaithersburg.

≈ *8* ≈

According to Gabe Watson, the current had been too strong.

His wife Tina was having difficulty. She jerked her thumb over her shoulder, signaling for them to go back toward a dive rope that would safely lead them to the surface. He thought they were in trouble.

She grabbed his right hand with her left as they continued to fight a fast moving tide that was pushing them further away from the wreck. Scared to death, he towed her back toward the dive rope. Gabe grabbed his air hose and motioned for her to put air into her buoyancy vest to help her ascend to the surface. Tina was now in a full blown panic.

Without warning, Gabe felt a whack across his face that knocked his mask and mouthpiece ajar. Forced to clear his mask and grab his backup "safe second" regulator, he let go of his grip on Tina — and lost her forever.

In the brief instant it took to get his mask back on, she was gone. Tina was now ten feet below him, sinking toward the ocean floor. Her arms were outstretched, reaching upward toward him, a helpless look on her face visible through her mask. Gabe attempted to kick after her, but she was plummeting beyond his ability to reach her.

No one expects to ever be forced to make the kind of split-second decision that Gabe made at that instant. It would be one that would haunt him forever.

He swam to find someone, anyone, stopping briefly to try and signal to an Asian diver to no avail. Quickly, he ascended to the surface and began yelling frantically for help.

Divers from the *Spoilsport* and another excursion boat, *Jazz II,* were oblivious to what was going on with Tina Watson. Divemaster Wade Singleton had already been underwater, seven minutes into his dive. He spotted someone obviously in trouble, lying face up just about 15 meters off the *Yongala*'s bow. Singleton kicked quickly downward to the motionless diver. It was Tina. Her eyes were open, but she wasn't breathing. He reached for the regulator still in her mouth and pressed the purge button, forcing air into her mouth. Holding her head back to help keep her airway open, Singleton dropped his dive weights then added air to his BCD to help him carry Tina to the surface, cradling her in his arms as they rose.

Even though he was aware a quick ascent could cause a fatal attack of the bends, Singleton brought Tina up from a depth of 30 meters in nearly a minute and a half. It was a risky and brave move; one he hoped would save her life.

Doctor Stanley Stutz, another diver on the trip, was only a few meters away as Singleton swam by him. Dr. Stutz could see Tina's eyes were wide open and vomit was trailing from her open mouth.

The *Jazz II* was the closest vessel. Singleton pulled Tina toward the boat's stern; its skipper leapt into the water to help Singleton bring her aboard. Several passengers attempted resuscitation. Tina expelled water and more vomit, but there were still no signs of life. Doctor John Downie, an emergency trauma surgeon who was another tourist diver on the trip, rushed to lend aid.

Gabe had been taken back to the *Spoilsport*. Tina was given CPR for 40 minutes. In the end, there was nothing that could be done.

When Doctor Downie told Gabe she was gone, the anguished husband collapsed, sobbing wildly.

Gabe claimed the problems he'd been having with his ears had prevented him from diving deeper to go after Tina. He also admitted that his rescue driver training hadn't really covered the proper way to get someone in trouble back to the surface.

There was just one problem with Gabe's story. Doctor Stanley Stutz had witnessed something very suspicious: Gabe's arms had been wrapped around Tina's back moments before she fell to the ocean floor.

≈ *9* ≈

According to prosecutors, FBI documents clearly outlined Gary Giordano's suspicious behavior in the days after Robyn vanished. Included were transcripts of Giordano's conversations with American Express regarding the accidental death policy he had taken out on Robyn Gardner just one day before the two had left for Aruba — the same policy she signed, naming him the beneficiary.

To those who suspected foul play, there clearly appeared to be one and a half million reasons for motive. It also appeared that Giordano wasted no time contacting Amex. Indeed, insurance representatives were growing increasingly skeptical about his claim; he seemed to act like someone more worried about his travel expenses than the life of his traveling companion. One Amex rep became so disturbed by a conversation with Giordano that he phoned both the police in Robyn's home town and authorities back in Aruba. In describing the conversation to the FBI, he said Giordano "sounded excited, like he was about to win something."

The transcripts also revealed Giordano telling an agent, "It's, you know, most likely a drowning."

Even more bizarre was the discovery of a second accidental death policy, one that Giordano had purchased for *another woman* only a month before going to Aruba with Robyn Gardner.

All of this sounded a bit too familiar for Carrie Emerson; she chose to now come forward with the story of her own bizarre encounter with Gary Giordano.

According to Carrie, it was her 17 year old daughter's dream to be a model and act in TV commercials — a dream that was bolstered by a phone call from Gary Giordano offering the underage girl a modeling gig.

Not just any modeling gig: one that was shooting in Aruba.

Carrie's daughter had been going by the stage name of "Taylor Tyler." Giordano had seen photos of "Taylor" on the Internet and tried to reach the young girl by phone. Instead, he ended up talking to Carrie, who was posing as "Taylor" to find out what this supposed job was all about. Charming and convincing, Giordano referred to himself not only as a "producer," but also as a professional manager and talent agent. He claimed that a model he had booked for a photo shoot in Aruba had backed out and was now offering Taylor $5,000 plus an all-expenses paid trip to the island if she would take the gig.

Taylor would have to come unsupervised. Giordano would look after her well-being and she would be protected.

"This won't turn into another Natalee Holloway thing." were the words she claimed Giordano used to reassure Taylor's safety.

Carrie stopped posing as "Taylor" and introduced herself as "Taylor's manager." Despite Giordano's spiel about the modeling job and the reassurances of Taylor's safety while alone in Aruba with him, Carrie rebuffed him. Though Taylor was legally an adult, Carrie was not going to allow her daughter to travel out of the country alone just for a job, especially one that sounded suspicious at best.

The next turn of the conversation seemingly justified that suspicion. According to Carrie, Giordano made a startling offer. "If you would like to come, I could get you a mother-daughter shoot for a bathing suit company." Giordano turned on the charm by telling Carrie that she was a gorgeous woman.

Yet according to Carrie, Giordano didn't even know her. Not only would he not take "no" for an answer, he upped the ante beyond any appearance of professionalism. "He said 'If you go with us and you sleep with me, I'll take care of you financially,'" claimed Carrie. "'I'll go you one better. I've always had a mother-daughter fantasy. If you both sleep with me, I'll take care of you financially for the rest of your life.'"

That offer was also met with understandable rejection, at which point Giordano "got very irate," said Carrie. "He told me that he could make me disappear and no one would ever look for me."

Later, she would tell reporters, "He (Giordano) made the offer sound so wonderful that anyone needing the money or the modeling job would have gone."

Robyn Gardner had recently lost her job as a dental assistant. Based on Carrie Emerson's story, speculation now arose: was it possible Robyn could have been enticed into taking a free trip to Aruba under a seemingly-shady pretense, just like the one Taylor Tylor's mother described on national TV?

This added more brushstrokes to the Gary Giordano portrait being painted by the media. Not just *if*, but *how* did Giordano somehow facilitate getting Robyn Gardner to take a trip with him to this island getaway, far outside the U.S., secreted away from prying eyes?

Yet another new revelation was about to clear up some of those questions, while at the same time make add another layer of confusion to the proceedings: the contents of Gary Giordano's digital camera.

≈ *10* ≈

The camera images were shocking and disturbing. A description by a source inside the investigation labeled them as "beyond pornographic."

Gary Giordano's camera, laptop and cell phone had been confiscated and sent to Curacao for closer examination. Investigators hoped to find clues that could prove their single suspect had brought Robyn Gardner to Aruba under false pretenses; those clues would, hopefully, also support the allegations that Giordano was directly involved with Robyn's disappearance.

Solicitor General Taco Stein stood in front of the daily throng of reporters from around the world. Sunglasses on, he confirmed Giordano's camera had been taken as potential evidence. There were indeed pictures of Robyn inside, taken during the trip. Though Taco Stein would refuse to comment on those images, a source would divulge their lurid nature.

Some showed Robyn naked, posing for the camera. Others taken by Giordano captured explicit acts of a sexual nature.

As Editor-in-Chief of Aruba's English-language newspaper *Aruba Today*, Julia Renfro had become a major source for American media during the Natalee Holloway investigation in 2005. Her description of the Robyn Gardner sex photos was simply chilling.

"You only see organs," she told one online gossip outlet. "You don't know if she is awake."

Following news of the lewd digital photos, word spread that Giordano was again refusing to cooperate with investigators. Aruban law allowed questioning of a suspect without attorneys present; however, even while subjected to interrogations that lasted up to six hours at a time inside his hot and stuffy cell, Giordano was saying nothing.

After more than two weeks in custody, Giordano had yet to be charged with a crime.

Prosecutors begged for an extension. Feeling that significant questions still remained open, authorities remanded Giordano to jail for an additional sixteen days, despite objections from his lawyer Michael Lopez.

"We cannot deduce that there is hard proof to sustain a demand by the public prosecutor against our client," Lopez told the media. While his lawyer made his appeal in the court of public opinion, Giordano was led back to KIA prison on the southern tip of the island, a striped shirt draped over his head to obscure his face from cameras.

The location was doubly ironic. KIA was the same facility where Joran van der Sloot had been detained while being questioned in the Natalee Holloway investigation. It was also within direct eyeshot of the very beach where Robyn Gardner had allegedly gone missing.

The integrity of Giordano's beach disappearance story continued to deteriorate. "People have drowned at Baby Beach before," Taco Stein said. "But in the last two years, bodies were found almost right away." Stein's investigations, in fact, refuted Giordano's claims that rough seas were to blame for pulling Robyn out with the current. "We checked the tide," said Stein. "When police came to investigate at 7 p.m. that evening, the sea was calm and no wind."

Meanwhile, in grueling Aruban heat that reached upwards of 104 degrees, students and instructors from the local police academy, along with a Red Cross specialist, continued to search the island's southern tip for any sign of Robyn. The Morning News reported:

A search team of approximately 40 stretched out over the scrub-laden shoreline beginning at Seroe Colorado, in the former Lago Colony, and examined the area along the northeastern shore as far as the Vader Piet Windmill Farm beginning at 8:00 AM yesterday morning. It was hard going over the landscape from the colony road to the shoreline consisting almost entirely of hard, sharp coral rock.

Back home in Maryland, Robyn's family issued a statement: "We are confident in the decision made by the Aruban authorities to keep Gary Giordano in custody, and we continue to be pleased with the way they have handled our daughter's case." The family offered their gratitude for the worldwide support and continued to hope Robyn was still alive.

Though rumors of Robyn travelling to Aruba as Giordano's paid escort became rampant, those close to her were steadfast in their insistence that this was not the case.

"I don't think she would have accepted money to go, or had done anything like that before," claimed Robyn's close friend, Reece Armstrong. She also couldn't believe that Robyn had gone on the trip with Giordano to model. "I think she just thought of it as a vacation."

There was no doubt amongst Robyn's friends that she had been in a funk since losing her dental assistant job. "She was going through a rough time and when you are in that state you do things in the spur of the moment, and a trip away to clear her head sounded good to her," Reece added.

Reece was also quite disturbed at the news about the insurance policy. "I don't think Robyn would sign anything like that, but I imagine if she were to sign something she would leave it to her family," she said. "It leaves a bad taste in my mouth."

When asked about her feelings on Giordano, Reece said, "I think he 100 percent has to do with why my friend isn't home right now."

Had Robyn Gardner, recently unemployed and reportedly despondent, really been desperate for money? Been *that* desperate? Certainly she was at the age when most models have long-since retired, much less attempted to start a new career. The hallowed industries of modeling and entertainment are littered with countless sad stories of gullible victims deceived by slick snake-oil salesmen who promised a fast-track to fulfilling one's dream.

Could the stresses in Robyn Gardner's life have emotionally compromised her ability to turn down a chance to change her life and reinvent herself — even if it were the kind of proposition that would normally and obviously seem too good to be true?

When asked by local media if the FBI was on the island, Taco Stein admitted there was one agent in Aruba, recently arrived from the closest outpost in Barbados. "He coordinates the assistance under the public requests from Aruba to the United States, called a legal *attaché*." Stein added "He is not actively involved in the investigation."

Stein was not expecting more FBI agents to arrive. In his opinion they already had "very capable people" just a phone call away in the Netherlands. Plus, cadaver dogs could be sent from the National Police Agency.

Though, he added, there weren't any plans to do so at the time.

Back in Maryland, Richard Forester continued to depict his relationship with Robyn as intimate and loving. By his accounts, they were a happy couple in love. That's why it seemed more than a bit odd to him how little Robyn had communicated in the days leading up to her disappearance: a handful of text messages, Facebook posts and voice and e-mails.

The few communications he did have were questionable at best and debatably false at worst.

She had obviously lied to him about her whereabouts during their last phone call — Forester was falsely led to believe she was in Florida, on vacation with her parents.

However, it turned out that the truth of Forester's statements was also debatable; it became apparent that there was more tension in his relationship with Robyn than Forester had originally led the media to believe.

During an episode of his CNN show, Dr. Drew Pinsky called into question Richard's relationship issues with Robyn. According to Pinsky, "(Forester) said 'Yes, we had a couple of fights, and I guess, the police got called once.' (Robyn) had a little problem with alcohol, maybe, but he didn't lead me to believe that there was anything wrong in their relationship or he claimed the fact, you know, that this was stunning, and he can't imagine that she was cheating on him."

Pinsky's guests that night included Reece Armstrong and Lianne Delawter, another friend of Robyn's. As television hosts probing a juicy story are wont to do, Pinsky tried to lure them into shedding more light on what was really going on between Forester and Robyn.

"You're her girlfriends. You know, she would confide in you things that maybe she wouldn't confide in her boyfriend, and we're all trying to make sense of why this woman would suddenly go with this guy and take off. Was she prone to that kind of thing? I mean, how do you make sense of all this?" prodded Pinsky.

Delawter wasn't taking the bait. If there was dirt to dish on Richard and Robyn, she wasn't going to offer a plateful. However, she was more than willing to make clear what she knew about Giordano's relationship with Robyn — including exactly how long Robyn had been keeping this secret from Forester.

"Well, I believe that Gary was a friend of Robyn's previous to this for a couple of years. So, it's not like you're just meeting some stranger and going away. She was going through a difficult time," Delawter said into the camera. "I just think that with everything that was going on in her life, she said, yes, sure I'll go."

"She never thought anything about it. It was just going away with a friend," added Delawter.

The image Robyn's friends had of her certainly didn't match up with the same Robyn who Giordano had allegedly photographed naked and engaged in sex acts.

Was boyfriend Richard Forester the only one Robyn Gardner was hiding the truth from? Her family certainly had no idea. Who, if anyone, really knew what was going on in her life?

Christina Jones was Robyn Gardner's roommate at the apartment they shared when Robyn wasn't staying at Forester's place. Jones had bonded with Robyn; they each had tattoos, which made them stand out in the small town where they lived. They each had faced the social stigma of being judged as "wild" despite Jones' assertion they were both actually quite mild.

So as a close friend and roommate, Jones was privy to otherwise hidden details of Robyn's life. She was able to pull back the curtain on what no one else seemed to know — Robyn and Giordano had been in a long on-again, off-again relationship.

According to Jones, they had a "roller coaster friendship…good one day and troubled the next." The pair would go out for drinks and be friendly for one period of time and then not speak to each other for another.

"Some months she wouldn't even see him and then other months he'd weasel his way back in," said Jones. "Sometimes Robyn was very focused on having a solid relationship with Richard when things were good, and then you wouldn't hear about Gary."

Jones made one thing very clear: she had raised serious objections after Robyn told her about the Aruba trip.

"She came to me and said, 'Hey, I'm going to Aruba,'" Jones said. "And then she said she was going with Gary, it became a 'why? Why? Are you sure?'"

Just a few months earlier Jones had been present when Giordano flipped out on Robyn via text message. He had invited her to go on a cruise with him. At first Robyn agreed, but then changed her mind and instead went to New York with Jones.

"He (Giordano) was texting her while we were at breakfast, very angry at her because she decided she wasn't going to go on the cruise," Jones told ABC News of the incident. "And his responses by text, which I don't feel comfortable repeating, were aggressive, harmful, something that doesn't sit right within myself."

Her words undeniably echoed the same sentiments expressed by the other women who had come forth concerning Giordano and his alleged nasty temper. If this hearsay was any indication, along with filed court documents concerning Giordano's ex-wife and girlfriends, there was indeed an ongoing pattern of angry, unsettling behavior by a man who did not take kindly to not getting his way with women.

Four weeks after Robyn's disappearance, the Aruban police filed an official report. Three witnesses claimed that on August 2, Giordano had approached them, saying, "Can you help me? We were snorkeling and my girlfriend is missing." This seemed to coincide with Giordano's accounting of the events.

However, there were a couple of odd discrepancies.

According to the police, several eyewitnesses told police Giordano seemed very calm, especially under the circumstances. One male witness in particular cited Giordano's behavior as "weird," and questioned why Giordano neither cried nor put any pressure on police to find his girlfriend.

Another woman echoed the description of Giordano's relaxed attitude and made even more damning observations: while Giordano's sneakers were wet, his shorts appeared dry.

"They were certainly not soaking wet because there was no water dripping from his pants. In my opinion, the man was covered in sweat," the eyewitness claimed according to the police report.

It was this same eyewitness, with the seemingly keen eye for detail, who told investigators she noticed *something else* that seemed rather curious: Gary Giordano had a cut on his throat. "It looked as if someone had scratched him with a nail," she said in her statement.

The same male witness who thought Giordano "weird" also told police he had seen blood on the beach. According to him, Giordano had a cut on his right shin, to which Giordano allegedly replied "No...that's my girlfriend, I wouldn't kill her."

Another female witness, who also saw the blood on Giordano, asked him about it. According to the police report, Giordano then said "No, no, no we were not fighting. We were cool all day. It was nothing like that."

They were cool. They were not fighting. He wouldn't kill her.

The eyewitness testimony raised curiosity in the police, who now also wanted to know how well Giordano got along with his "girlfriend." When questioned, Giordano answered that the couple "enjoyed each other" and "there was no reason to argue."

This "sunshine and roses" portrayal of their relationship contradicted those given by Robyn's friends. Specifically, the description ran counter to the one from Robyn's roommate, Christina Jones, who clearly defined their "roller coaster friendship."

Security camera footage would also allegedly tell a different story.

≈ *11* ≈

According to a source close to the investigation, a closed-circuit camera videotape showing Robyn and Giordano in the midst of a heated fight was obtained from the Marriott Resort where the pair was staying. It was an argument made more significant by one fact: it occurred on the same day Robyn vanished.

"They were having a major fight. Robyn was waving her arms and shouting at Giordano. He was grabbing her arms and jerking her around and shouting back at her," reported the source. "Then Giordano apparently realized their argument was heating up in public where someone might overhear them. He violently grabbed the back of Robyn's neck with one hand and shoved her back into the elevator with the other hand."

Though the soundless surveillance video didn't betray what was actually said between the two, the source would drop another bombshell to reporters

— an alleged lip-reading analysis of the argument claiming that Robyn had yelled, "I'm out of here. I'm leaving. I'm not spending another minute with you!" to which Giordano purportedly responded "Get back here! I'll kill you!"

Authorities never confirmed this finding. However, it begs the question: why would Giordano state to the authorities that he had "no reason to argue" when video surveillance proved he had done just that? Forgetfulness? Or conveniently leaving out a fact he thought would never surface otherwise?

Despite continuing objections by Giordano's attorney that all of this evidence was purely circumstantial and did not directly implicate his client in any wrongdoing, the court found otherwise.

On August 31, *The Aruba Herald* published the following:

The Examining Magistrate has ruled today that the American man G.V.G., suspected of involvement in the possible drowning of the American woman R.G. on the 2nd of august 2011, will remain in custody for a period of sixty (60) more days.

This was done on request of the Prosecutor's Office Aruba. The Prosecutor's Office and the Aruban Police Force hereby once more urge people who can give any information about the suspect G.V.G. to contact the Aruban Police in person or via the special tip line 11141.

"I feel that justice is starting to be served," Robyn's friend Lianne Delawter told one online gossip outlet. "If he gets released, it takes us further away from the truth and we may never know what happened."

The announcement came one day after Gary Giordano's father Frank had spoken to reporters in an effort to combat the mounting negative press. To Frank, Gary was "not a monster, but a good human being who is good to his family."

80 year-old Frank Giordano stood alone in public defense of his son's character. He released family snapshots of a smiling Gary Giordano during happier times. Frank insisted the insinuations about Gary were untrue. "I know he would not be able to kill someone. To murder someone."

At that time, according to family members, Frank was suffering from cancer. The devastating toll the chemotherapy was taking on his frail body was nothing compared to the strain of seeing what was happening to his son in such a public manner.

Delawter was sympathetic to Giordano's father. "He was being honest and truthful and I don't think he knew anything. What person says 'I'm a sexual stalker,' to his dad?"

Continuing to confound the story, yet more rumors began to emerge. One magazine reported that Robyn and Giordano's relationship had *not* begun on Match.com, the same online matchmaking site where she and Forester had first met. According to one of Robyn's friends, the pair had instead connected through *Adult Friend Finder*, a site known to bill itself as the world's largest meeting place for swingers.

There were also additional allegations about Robyn's drinking. "It wasn't anything her friends worried about. Everyone drinks, especially on holiday," said Delawter.

However, one witness claimed he had seen a heavily intoxicated Robyn Gardner just two hours before her disappearance. Images of her, first shown on ABC News, were initially reported as having come from surveillance cameras. The two photos showed Robyn and Giordano leaving the Rum Reef Bar & Grill at 4:12 p.m. Robyn was wearing black sunglasses, high heels and a multi-colored striped sundress — the same dress later positively identified "with 100 percent certainty" by Forester as Robyn's favorite. Both she and Giordano were carrying blue plastic cups, described by witnesses as containing vodka and orange juice.

Though the actual contents of those plastic cups were a mystery, the truth about the two images of Robyn Gardner was not; they hadn't come from a surveillance camera at all. According to a source, the images had been taken from a Blackberry. The shooter had been a random stranger at the bar who just wanted a few discreet pictures of Robyn.

If anything, by virtue of being a sexy blonde, Robyn Gardner cut a noticeable and memorable figure.

While there was nothing unusual about the pair's demeanor in the images, eyewitnesses reported that Robyn seemed "woozy: and had no appetite, barely eating the salad she had ordered. Giordano's behavior also struck one waiter as rather odd. After being seated, Giordano jumped up to make introductions, making a point to identify himself and his companion. "My name is Gary and this is Robyn and we're from Maryland."

Witnesses believed the pair was indeed in some kind of romantic relationship. The server even claimed Robyn once referred to Giordano as her "husband."

But it would be a different worker at the Rum Reef Bar & Grill who would make additional damning allegations. According to the server's statement, the very same Gary Giordano would return to the restaurant some twelve hours after reporting Robyn missing. However, this time Giordano's companion would be an attorney, and Giordano would appear "indifferent" to the disappearance of the woman he had constantly referred to as his "girlfriend."

Giordano, upon being questioned about Robyn's inebriation at the restaurant, told authorities the pair had been drinking vodka back at the Marriott Resort before heading out to the Rum Reef Bar & Grill. He also revealed that Robyn had taken sleeping pills earlier in the day.

The original police search of the pair's Marriott Hotel room had indeed turned up the sleep medication Ambien.

Richard Forester, however, scoffed at these claims. Not only was Robyn not the type to ever go snorkeling for fear of messing up her carefully done hair extensions, make-up and spray tan, she was not the type to take Ambien.

"I've never known Robyn to take any sleeping pills in the middle of the day," he told ABC News.

"Nor do I know why anybody would take sleeping pills in the middle of the day."

Forester not only questioned the story's legitimacy, he also doubted the absolute logic behind the actions. "You say she was taking sleeping pills, then you give her vodka? And then you take her snorkeling? Really? Why would anybody do that?"

Forester remained publicly adamant that Giordano was hiding the truth. "Obviously," he said, "I don't believe anything he's saying."

≈ *12* ≈

As circumstantial evidence, an inconsistent story, and some serious character issues continued to mount against Gary Giordano, new witness statements actually supported his account of events.

One source claimed seeing Robyn go into the water at Baby Beach where she gashed her toe during her initial attempt to go swimming. Her toe bleeding, she exited from the water. A spot of blood was detected in the parking area behind the restaurant near where Giordano had parked the rental Toyota Rav-4.

The source also said two sharks and a giant sea turtle were spotted by helicopters in the same area at around the same time Robyn allegedly vanished.

Then a major news network reported that there was indeed an eyewitness present when Gardner signed the travel insurance form naming Giordano as beneficiary. The witness claimed that Robyn actually appeared to be coherent at the time of the signing.

Even as Gary Giordano became somewhat vindicated, the mother-daughter duo who had claimed Giordano wanted to take them both to Aruba — 18 year old Taylor Tyler and her mother Carrie Emerson — were coming under attack. After appearing on Nancy Grace's TV show, public opinions were voiced that the mother-daughter duo were pulling some kind of fast one on the media. Carrie's own modeling headshots and photos were discovered by one Internet news site — but that wasn't all. There were allegations that Carrie had pushed her daughter into modeling at too young of an age. When "Taylor" was only 14, Carrie signed a contract allowing her daughter to pose in sexy lingerie on the now-defunct daphneguurl.com, a membership-only site for discerning adults over 18 years of age.

If that wasn't enough, an anonymous commenter claiming to know the mother-daughter duo posted allegations that Carrie Emerson was a con-artist known as "Catfishin' Carrie." Though most anonymous Internet commenting is (rightfully) subject to much skepticism, this particular commenter detailed how to find record of Carrie's criminal past in the official online pubic database of Virginia's judicial system.

According to the Commonwealth of Virginia, on December 6, 2007, a female named Carrie T. Emerson from Chester, VA, described as a "White Caucasian (Non-Hispanic)," was found guilty in the Chesterfield County General District Court of misdemeanor solicitation of prostitution and fined a lofty $100. Just over two months later, the same Carrie T. Emerson (now listed as being from Doswell, VA) was popped for pickpocketing and destruction of property.

While none of Carrie's critics, at any time, disputed the claims of her personal Gary Giordano story, her detractors felt a sense that she was using Robyn's disappearance and Giordano's notoriety as an excuse to gain media attention. It was also alleged, within the same comment thread, that Carrie had not been around for most of her daughter's life and that "Taylor" had worked as a stripper during her senior year of high school.

As the outlying stories around Robyn's disappearance continued to expand and get more bizarre, back in Maryland Richard Forester remained outspoken in his criticism of Gary Giordano. Though admittedly shaken and hurt to discover Robyn had gone on an apparently romantic getaway with another man — especially one of noticeably questionable character — he continued to tell the media "All that matters is getting her home, and then for justice to be served, whatever it has to be…nothing else matters."

Forester was coming under constant fire for not having gone to Aruba as a grieving boyfriend likely would. Some questioned why he was choosing to stay put and watch from the sidelines. "I'd love to go down there and help, but I'm best serving her here," he told one online gossip outlet. He also expressed a continuing complaint that the search for Robyn hadn't begun earlier and that, as far as he knew, the Aruban authorities hadn't used dogs to track her scent.

Giordano, meanwhile, remained behind bars in a sweltering cell at KIA Prison. Even though he faced daily interrogation, the case against him was going nowhere.

As investigators continued to follow the trail of travel receipts, one thing was clear: starting with four Bloody Marys ordered at 9 a.m. at the Orlando Airport before boarding their Aruba flight, Giordano and Robyn had consumed a notable amount of alcohol during their trip. After checking into the Marriott, the pair purchased a liter of Ciroq vodka and took it back to their shared room.

Alcohol consumption led to another seeming inconsistency in Giordano's story. He and Robyn had not purchased drinks at the Rum Reef Bar & Grill the afternoon of August 2, even though there were reports they were seen carrying cups full of vodka and orange juice. Local fisherman and alleged eyewitness Sergio Silva was now telling folks that Giordano appeared to be extremely drunk at the time he had seen them. In fact, Silva would later contend that the reason Giordano went back to his room shortly after police arrived was because he was so drunk the cops couldn't talk to him.

Police were entertaining a theory that Giordano had fantasized that Robyn was indeed his "girlfriend" and believed she was in love with him. After seeing the messages she sent to Forester from her iPad, Giordano flew into a jealous rage and killed her.

According to another source, police were also checking into a theory that the hypothetical murder was committed in Seroe Colorado, a nearby housing area with fifty empty shacks that were once home to oil workers. The refinery was now defunct, making the abandoned Seroe Colorado an opportune location to have beaten, strangled or otherwise tortured Robyn to death far away from prying eyes.

Gary Giordano's suspiciously calm demeanor after reporting Robyn's disappearance, the same calm behavior often mentioned by the women who publicly spoke of their fear of Giordano, played perfectly into the police's theory. During those initial hours of their search, Giordano reportedly looked down at his watch at one point and calmly told police "She might be dead now."

On September 1, 2011, the day after Giordano was ordered to spend an additional sixty days behind bars, Joran van der Sloot — the prime suspect in the unsolved Natalee Holloway disappearance — was being charged with murder, thousands of miles away in a Peruvian court. Joran had taken the victim, 21 year-old Stephany Flores, back to his hotel room in Lima. He had later flown into a rage and killed her with his bare hands after she had used his computer to look up his involvement in the Holloway case. The murder occurred, ironically, on the fifth anniversary of the day Natalee Holloway vanished from the same beach town of Oranjestad.

The cases, though separate, were similar and connected enough that Giordano's attorney

Michael Lopez feared his client was being unfairly tarnished by the public's continuing outcry that justice had never been served for Natalee Holloway. Despite copious amounts of circumstantial evidence in the Holloway case, Joran van der Sloot was allowed to walk for one important reason: a body was never found. Lopez argued (again) that there was not enough evidence to warrant Giordano's continued detention and he should be set free for the same reason — no body.

A judge felt otherwise and Lopez's objection was overruled. The following Wednesday a three-judge panel upheld the ruling; Giordano would remain in jail at least until the end of October.

Yet two months later, despite keeping their main suspect behind bars, the search for answers finally ground to a halt. Aruban authorities made a rather unusual public plea — they begged for anyone with information to come forth. If it wasn't clear before, without a smoking gun, Giordano could walk. The prosecution was desperate.

≈ 13 ≈

Doctor Stanley Stutz had witnessed something very suspicious. Stutz told Townsville police that he had seen Gabe cradling Tina, his arms wrapped around her as she struggled. He added, "It happened so fast I am not sure."

"I then saw them both split apart. I saw Diver 2 (Gabe) got to the surface really quickly," claimed Stutz. "I saw Diver 1 (Tina) begin to sink toward the sea bed."

Though it took almost five years, the Australian coroner in Townsville finally believed there was enough evidence of guilt to pursue a murder conviction for Gabe Watson. To no one's surprise, the pathologist had positively identified the cause of death as drowning.

In the official inquest, Townsville coroner David Robert Glasgow testified to the following:

Mr. Thomas' (Tina's Father's) evidence is that he discussed with Tina shortly prior to her marriage to Gabe,

Gabe's request that she not only increase her Company insurance to the maximum but make him the beneficiary. Mr. Thomas said that it was resolved that Tina would tell Gabe that such had been done. Evidence was also given by Company officers of Gabe's inquiry to the company about Tina's insurance after her death. I am of the view Mr. Thomas' evidence would be admissible in criminal proceedings against Gabe and may be such to provide a possible motive.

Opportunity and motive were certainly definable in the case of Tina Watson's death. If a big insurance payout, possibly $1 million, was in the offing, the coroner was confident they could prove Gabe premeditated her murder in order to cash in. It was a damning accusation, one that began to grow in grieving father Tommy Thomas' mind not too long after that fateful day.

Tina's father would never forget the events. He had just arrived at work. Gabe's dad was on the phone, bearing the worst news any father could possibly ever receive. The story surrounding Tina's tragic honeymoon death half a world away crushed Tommy. Gabe's father apologized; Gabe had not been able to emotionally pull himself together to make the call himself.

It was nightfall by the time Tommy finally reached Gabe by phone in the cheap hotel room Mike Ball Expeditions had begrudgingly booked for him. Tommy was joined by Tina's mother Cindy and her sister Alanda on different handsets at the Watson House. Gabe told them he had held Tina while the doctors and other passengers tried to resuscitate her.

They had no idea that Gabe hadn't told them the truth.

Tina's body began the trek home over a week later, on November 1, 2003. Gabe and his mother, who had flown halfway around the world to be with her son, boarded a flight carrying Tina's body to New Zealand on one of the many legs of the long journey home to Alabama. During the plane's descent into Auckland, Gabe complained of acute ear pain. Seven days prior, on October 25, a Townsville doctor had diagnosed Gabe with a case of barotrauma, a condition caused by subjecting the eardrum to sudden pressure differences. Taken right from the plane by ambulance to Auckland City Hospital, Gabe was examined by Dr. David Scott who, despite being primarily an anesthetist by trade, deemed there to be no further damage to Gabe's ears.

When the plane carrying Tina's casket finally arrived back home, some suspected that Gabe had conjured the episode of ear pain to avoid facing Tina's father at the airport.

Tina's funeral was an uncomfortable affair for both families. Gabe's parents and Tina's parents never seemed to click. Tommy and Cindy Thomas had never quite warmed up to Gabe. Tommy found the boy to be aloof and a bit odd — an incompatible choice of a husband for his vivacious and outgoing daughter. The Thomases did little to be welcoming. When once asked to dinner by Gabe's parents, Cindy reportedly responded, "Why? Tina is marrying into your family. We're not."

Some of Tina's family and friends noted that Gabe made insensitive and inappropriate comments at the funeral. Tina's best friend Amanda Phillips later claimed that, when she and Gabe went up to Tina's open casket together, Gabe commented about Tina that "at least her breasts look perky."

Gabe denied ever saying such a thing.

One thing Gabe did do was to put an envelope into Tina's casket before it was closed. He also removed Tina's engagement ring and slipped it into his pocket. Others found Gabe's overall lack of emotion odd. Gabe told them he had cried all he could cry back in Australia.

After Tina was laid to rest, a small wake was held at the home of Gabe's parents. Video and photos of the honeymoon where shown to those in attendance. Sadly, some displayed Australian signs warning of dangerous animals.

Over time Tommy would start to believe that the most dangerous animal of all was Gabe. His concerns were given voice by a surprise phone call from a pair of expert divers who were on the *Spoilsport* the day Tina died. They believed Gabe's story was suspicious.

Authorities back in Australia had looked into the circumstances surrounding Tina's death. Eyewitnesses had been interviewed, Tina had been autopsied and her gear, including her dive computer, had all been examined. Townsville police interrogated Gabe twice in the days following the incident. After their preliminary investigation, Tina's drowning was officially ruled an accident.

However, after being told what these other eyewitnesses believed, Tommy and Cindy Thomas were now convinced Gabe was directly to blame. From their family home they began lobbying the Queensland Police and Queensland government, as well as Alabama Police, to investigate Tina's death as a murder.

≈ *14* ≈

Robyn Gardner had been missing from Aruba for a month. Roommate Christine Jones had flown to Aruba with Robyn's cousin, Kelly Colson, because a psychic had told her that Robyn's body was not at sea, but instead buried close to shore.

On the island, Christina and Kelly were met by a news crew from NBC's Today Show.

"There's just so much to cover." Christina Jones was obviously overwhelmed and on the verge of tears behind her dark sunglasses. "I feel so helpless," the tattooed brunette told the correspondent as they stood on Baby Beach within sight of KIA prison where Giordano was being held.

"This isn't an accident," Christina said. "Robyn is missing, murdered. That guy in that jail is the only guy that knows where she is and he's lying. We all know he's lying."

Christina desperately drove around the island hoping to find a clue that would lead them to Robyn. The psychic hadn't given them an exact location, only the suggestion that Robyn was in a swampy area underneath something, and that a piece of fabric found with her would solve the puzzle.

"She was going through a rough time," Christina said of Robyn. "I was like the big sister. I'm still the big sister trying to find her. She's a great person and her smile, it would light up the room."

Later that same night, Christina Jones chatted with a different psychic, Carla Baron, via Skype. Baron, a well-known psychic profiler who had been featured on TV several times, performed a reading over the video chat. "My read provided many more details on the event itself, and points surrounding where I saw Robyn's body. I also was able to get some sense that there was an accomplice present with Gary Giordano," Baron wrote later in her blog about the session.

The National Enquirer dropped a bombshell allegation a couple of days later. The American supermarket tabloid had earned an infamous reputation of paying for tips and printing questionable headlines; it was also the first "news source" to break the scandal of one-time Presidential candidate John Edwards' secret love child with a former campaign staffer. The Robyn Gardner case was right up their alley.

The tabloid reported that, according to sources, the guards at the San Nicolas police station jail, where Giordano was first held, were now claiming to have heard their prime suspect crying and banging his fists against the concrete walls of his cell while screaming, "It's all my fault!"

Giordano was said to cry out in his sleep, his voice wracked with guilt. "Robyn! I'm so sorry! Forgive me!" "Jesus, help me! I'm so, soooo sorry!"

Even more damning were incriminating comments Giordano allegedly made to other inmates at San Nicholas. "How much of a sentence can I get if they suspect I killed her but they can't find proof and can't find her body," claimed the source.

≈ 15 ≈

Connie Klein, Giordano's second wife, was informed of her ex-husband's sixty day sentence by a reporter from an online gossip website.

"This is the first I'm hearing about this," said Klein, now a real estate agent in Charlotte, North Carolina. According to Klein, she had been in contact with Giordano since his initial in Aruba and he was very concerned about the accusations against him. Beyond that, she refused to comment. Her silence was an attempt to keep her life with Gary Giordano where it belonged — in the past.

Wed for only two years, theirs was not a drama-free marriage. Police records from Cornelius, North Carolina reveal a disturbing 2007incident. After drunkenly returning home from a restaurant, Giordano's behavior had turned explosive. A heated argument erupted between the couple, during which Giordano smashed a cake in the couple's kitchen before storming out of the house.

When police arrived, Giordano was found at a neighbor's house. The responding officers told him that he should stay there until things cooled down.

Giordano and Klein divorced in 2008. He left their home in North Carolina and moved back to Maryland. But his destructive behavior made the move with him: the drinking, the aggressive behavior. Each time another woman from Gary Giordano's past would open up to reporters, their stories sounded more and more like warning echoes. History continued repeating itself, continued to cloak Giordano in a cloud of suspicion.

Perhaps it was this same sense of pattern of behavior that made the surfacing of a yet another new video all that more chilling. Grainy security camera footage shot the day before Giordano reported Robyn missing shows the pair leaving the exact same bar, at almost the exact same time in the afternoon they would visit the next day. In the video Robyn is wearing the exact same sundress seen in the Blackberry snapshots from the following day.

Investigators considered this as more than just a case of returning for the conch chowder. This opened up the possibility that Giordano was casing the joint; it also begged the likelihood that he and Robyn were purposely seen together in order to cement his alibi. Outrageous theory or not, the prosecution was sniffing out any conceivable scenario that would pin Giordano to a crime.

Sensing the serious continuation of dogged pursuit, especially in the face of ongoing detention (and despite any official charges being filed against him), Giordano lawyered up in the United States. His new attorney was already famous with the tabloids for representing notorious child murder trial mom Casey Anthony — and getting her acquitted.

The Casey Anthony verdict had shocked many. Thus Attorney Jose Baez was no stranger to controversial clients already convicted in the court of public opinion. On Wednesday, September 14, 2011, Baez flew down to Aruba to help with his client's defense and serve as an advisor to Giordano's Aruban lawyer, Michael Lopez.

One person who clearly wasn't impressed was Richard Forester. He called Baez's hiring a "publicity stunt" — not for Giordano, but for Baez himself. Baez, who would later write the tell-all book "Presumed Guilty - Casey Anthony: the Inside Story," was considered by some to be nothing more than a self-aggrandizing media whore. Forester appeared to be a member of that group, considering the very concept a bad joke. It was his opinion that Baez didn't win the Casey Anthony case, but instead it was the prosecution who had lost it.

A great deal of press being written about Robyn's disappeared was published by gossip-oriented news sources, and they led the charge in establishing tone and tenor for the public's consumption. Every new rumor was treated with a fresh coat of sensationalism as each lurid tale played out around the world. It was story painting with a wide brush, and by nature it lost the nuances in each individual's unique character.

The dark side of Gary Giordano's personality dominated the public's image of him. If he had been a fictional character in a movie, he would be the moustache-twirling villain instantly recognizable as up to no good.

The story coverage also overlooked a certain level of character assassination of Robyn Gardner herself. Flirty, possibly vain, she was now subject to a subtle media overtone that gave her the reputation as some kind of a wild child. Here was a girl who liked to have a good time, replete with tattoos, insinuations of swinger websites, and "sneaky drinking," Robyn Gardner was no vestal virgin, but she certainly didn't deserve to have anything bad happen to her. The truth, as always, lay somewhere in between.

The various translations of the story also largely disregarded Robyn's intention for going to Aruba with Gary Giordano in the first place. Was she indeed just a doe-eyed victim led into a deadly sex trap outside of the country?

Aruban authorities were running out of time — and ideas — to establish a case against Giordano. Police were hoping a reenactment of the hours surrounding Robyn's disappearance would yield something they could grab and hold. Reconstructing Robyn's last movements would involve eyewitness testimony and surveillance video. Giordano, who had been asked several times to participate in such an exercise, declined through his lawyer. Giordano knew that what the police were really searching for was a better handle on the inconsistencies in his account of the events.

≈ 16 ≈

On September 20 around 4 p.m., at the same rocky beach where Robyn vanished, the police began retracing her steps using approximately the same timeline from the day in question. The two officers chosen to portray Robyn and Giordano made for convincing stunt doubles. With her long dyed-blond locks and dark sunglasses, the female officer they picked looked eerily like Robyn Gardner, right down to the similar-patterned sundress she wore. The officer playing Giordano's doppelganger was of similar height and build, even wearing the same kind of sneakers and swim trunks. For two and a half hours a team of over forty investigators and attorneys ran through various scenarios, including bringing key eyewitnesses back to the scene. The police looked for any shred of evidence to prove there was no way Giordano's story made sense.

Police parked a white Toyota Rav-4, simulating Giordano's rental car, right next to the Rum Reef

Bar & Grill. The actors walked along the shoreline, even stopping to pull on snorkels and briefly go into the surf. It was along this rocky beach where Robyn had cut her foot on jagged stone before supposedly returning to the water.

Investigators next recreated Giordano's alleged dash for help from the beach to the bar. One thing didn't quite dovetail with this recreation: surveillance video from August 2. On the day Robyn disappeared, Giordano is seen on tape walking at what would appear to be an unconcerned pace, not running. While the reenactment didn't necessarily prove anything, it did underscore what appeared to be yet another inconsistency in Giordano's version of events.

One person who wasn't happy about the re-enactment was Giordano himself. Jose Baez called the exercise "one sided," saying that parts of his client's story were ignored during the simulation. Baez also criticized Aruban authorities' refusal to videotape the proceedings, claiming they were being unfair to his client.

The reenactment did reveal two more photos — both quite mundane compared to the nearly pornographic images from Giordano's digital camera. In one shot Robyn was seen alone, wearing the same dress she had on during the last day she had been seen alive. The second shot she posed with Giordano, and it's the casual nature of this picture that makes it so noteworthy.

Goofy expressions and drunken smiles on both Robyn's and Giordano's faces betray any suspicion that she was in Aruba against her will. The photo, taken July 31, makes the pair look like any other fun-loving couple having a good time over a few vacation drinks. On the left side, Robyn cocks her head, seducing the camera with a sexy gaze. Close next to her, Giordano displays a daffy, open-mouthed grin almost making it appear that he had photobombed the shot.

The same day as the reenactment, Jose Baez took to the offensive. On ABC's "Good Morning America" he addressed the suspicion about the notorious $1.5 million insurance policy. Truth was, Baez said to the national TV audience, that Robyn Gardner also took out her own insurance policy for the trip.

"The two of them had policies on each other," stated Baez. "Now, of course, since Gary was paying for the trip, Gary was the beneficiary of Robyn's policy." In the policy covering Giordano, it was Giordano's mother who was his beneficiary.

Baez also dismissed the claim that these were life insurance policies. According to him, they were travel insurance. "So what this covers is medical, dental, car rental and a whole slew of other things," Baez added. "…including accidental death."

Baez was trying to throw cold water on what many felt was THE motive for Robyn Gardner's suspected killer. "Every time Mr. Giordano has traveled this year, whether it's been with Robyn Gardner or other individuals, he, in fact, had another companion he traveled with, he got the same insurance," said Baez. To hear him tell it, buying the type of policy to insure against out of pocket costs for unforeseen flight delays and medical care was not a suspicious act at all, but something mundane that smart travelers do all the time.

Though Baez was able to create an image of a man whose actions had been misinterpreted because of the accidental circumstances that followed, not everyone was ready to drop their suspicions. According to a report on ABC News, an Amex insurance agent was now saying that Giordano expressed an unusual urgency to make sure that the policy was filed before the trip. The agent claimed no other customer she had dealt with had mailed a hard copy of the policy form and faxed over a version as well.

If Giordano had bought travel insurance for other travel companions, it would definitely have established an explainable pattern of behavior. However, Baez would still have trouble smoothing over public opinions concerning the speed at which Giordano contacted Amex after Gardner went missing. While his lawyer was playing up the lack of a financial motive for murder, Gary Giordano's actual financial situation was falling under growing scrutiny.

≈ *17* ≈

The effort by Tina Watson's parents to have their daughter's honeymoon drowning death investigated as a murder was gaining steam. Lobbying on their behalf were a U.S. Congressman and a U.S Senator, as well as their local police chief.

In June of 2004 another detective from the Townsville Criminal Investigation Branch was appointed to review the case. The directive from above made it clear this was to be handled as a criminal matter rather than an accident investigation.

Eyewitnesses were interviewed again. This time, authorities dug deeper, managing to track down the taxi driver who had driven Gabe and Tina to the *Spoilsport*. Even several months after the fact, the cabbie alleged to remember that Gabe and Tina, though newlyweds, did not hold hands in the cab.

In late September of 2006, police went out to the *Yongala* to re-enact the fateful dive. They picked a day that they hoped could replicate the conditions from when Tina died. Though the September currents were running in the opposite direction, they proceeded with the exercise using a male police diver as a stand in for Tina. Through repeated dives, the results of the reenactment were not matching up to the story Gabe was telling.

Suspicions quickly surrounded the alleged malfunction of Gabe's dive computer. According to Gabe, he and Tina had to go back to the *Spoilsport* because the device was beeping since the battery was in backwards. Investigators determined two things. First, an upside-down battery would leave the computer shut off and completely unable to emit any beeping at all. Second, that meant the story was a ruse on Gabe's part in order to separate he and Tina from the dive group so they could be alone.

Based on the findings of the *Yongala* reenactment and the damning testimony of Dr. Stutz, authorities were painting a new picture of Gabe Watson. Allegations from other *Spoilsport* passengers that Gabe had been playing cards on the voyage back to Townsville suggested an indifferent, if callous attitude toward his wife's sudden death. There was no doubt in their minds that if Gabe was capable of lying to Tina's parents about being on the boat with her when desperate attempts were being made to resuscitate her, then he was capable of lying about the entire story.

All their evidence pointed to Gabe reaching around Tina's back and shutting off her air tank valve, holding her struggling body until she fell unconscious, then turning the air back on to hide the crime and letting her lifeless form drift to the sea floor.

A diver as inexperienced as Tina stood no chance of being able to turn her air tank back on. As a trained rescue diver, Gabe had to know this.

Plus, according to Tommy Thomas, there was a million dollars in motive thanks to Tina's life insurance policy that Gabe wanted changed in order to become the sole beneficiary.

It was almost the perfect murder.

By August of 2008 Gabe Watson had remarried. His new bride, schoolteacher Kim Lewis, had been introduced to the widower years after Tina's death. Three months later, Gabe would be indicted in the Townsville Supreme Court for Tina's murder. On May 13, 2009, Gabe voluntarily flew back to Australia to face the charges against him. He was arrested upon landing in Brisbane and remanded into custody.

Less than a month later, Gabe pleaded guilty — but not to murder.

Instead, Gabe Watson copped a plea to a much lesser offense. By admitting he allowed his wife to drown, Watson pleaded guilty to criminal negligence, an offense that still carried with it the option of life in jail. Nobody was prepared for what would happen at Gabe's sentencing, least of all Tina's parents.

Character issues continued to plague Gary Giordano in the public eye. His version of the events of August 2 was seemingly riddled with inconsistencies. The toupee wasn't helping him either. Because it was so obvious, the hairpiece became a focal point of some of the criticism of his character.

What else was Gary Giordano hiding?

Criminal records would reveal more. Aside from being the owner of a Maryland temporary staffing company run from his $1.3 million stone mansion in Gaithersburg, Giordano had been arrested twice in 2003 for theft. On March 11 he had been picked up for shoplifting jewelry from a Costco, then again in April for stealing from local Target stores in Frederick and Montgomery counties.

Oddly, this wasn't just a case of taking a pair of socks or a toothbrush. Giordano would brazenly pile up entire shopping carts with merchandise and then just roll the goods out the doors without paying. Sometimes, after loading his car with his ill-gotten goods, he'd go back into the Target and repeat the whole thing all over again.

According to authorities, Giordano would then use the Internet to fence stolen electronics such as video game systems and DVD players.

A master criminal he was not. On April 29, Giordano was eventually was busted trying to steal more electronic goods at a Germantown Target store. Police charged him with four counts of "theft over $500." Giordano posted bond and was released awaiting trial. By late August the whole matter would be over; Giordano copped a guilty plea to one count of theft in exchange for having the other three counts dropped. His sentence was suspended and he was allowed to walk.

Montgomery County Detective David Hill recalled the case many years later, specifically his memories of Giordano's demeanor. According to Hill, Giordano avoided conflict, choosing to run away from security rather than becoming combative. "He was an easy going guy. He wasn't a jerk."

Nonetheless, Hill's recollection of Giordano also included a certain sense of suspicion. "He would talk to us, but he seemed like he was a step ahead of us. He didn't want to give us any information."

Back in Aruba, Robyn Gardner had been missing for weeks and the official police investigation had remained squarely and only on Giordano. It wouldn't be until the second week of

September that new eyewitness testimony reignited a discarded theory: Giordano had an accomplice.

A second man, a white American, approximately 40 years of age with dark curly hair with two tattoos (a large heart over a cross on his left arm and unspecified ink on his left hand) had allegedly been seen talking to Robyn for ten minutes on the day she vanished.

This mystery man, purported to have been wearing brand new Nike sneakers, pricey sunglasses and a light-colored muscle shirt, arrived at the Rum Reef Bar & Grill just after Robyn and Giordano first entered on the afternoon of August 2. He took off shortly after they left. Though police and the FBI instituted an island-wide manhunt, the mystery man was never found or identified.

This idea of an accomplice led investigators to revisit their theory that, in the two hours between being seen at the Rum Reef Bar & Grill and reporting Robyn missing, Giordano in fact drove his intended victim to the abandoned oil refinery shacks of Seroe Colorado, killed her, and then hid her body in a shallow grave. Investigators theorized that the plan involved waiting until Giordano left the island, after which the mystery accomplice would retrieve Robyn's buried remains and dispose of them at sea. If there was such a man, and if Giordano had met him on one of the swingers websites he frequented, it would go a long way toward proving that Robyn's murder was premeditated for the sole purpose of collecting on her insurance policy.

One thing was for certain: according to even Giordano's own account, he was having serious financial woes. In January of 2011, despite owning his own company and living in a home valued at more than a million dollars, Giordano had petitioned in Montgomery County family court to lower the child support payments he was making to his first wife, Sharon. When his support payments had originally been set, Giordano was reporting a monthly income of $4,827 (approximately $58,000 a year). The judge ordered Giordano to pay Sharon $616 per month.

Citing a "material change in circumstances," Giordano submitted 2010 financial records indicating his earnings were "significantly lower than the figure used for calculating support at the last hearing."

At the same time, Giordano was also suing his second wife, Connie Klein for $6,757. Giordano had previously filed a suit against Klein in 2007 for $11,461; that case had been dismissed with prejudice less than a year later.

In May of 2011, Montgomery County District Court Judge Ronald B. Rubin denied Giordano's request for a reduction in his child support payments.

Giordano's luck in court had been less than stellar. In 2009 he attempted to sue Costco for $5,000, citing he had been subject to unlawful imprisonment during his 2003 arrest for shoplifting at their Frederick County store.

Judgment was found for the defendant. Costco won.

Despite those legal setbacks, perhaps the most humiliating legal defeat Giordano suffered came at the hands of Thomas D. Murphy, a former president of the Maryland State Bar Association. In January 2010 Giordano brought a $5 million lawsuit against another staffing company for breach of contract. He claimed that in 2007 he placed an employee at federal home mortgage lender Freddie Mac and was never compensated by the staffing company.

Murphy represented the staffing company in court. He confronted Giordano, accusing him of forging documents in the case, including the contract in question.

Court papers show that an executive with the staffing company claimed his wife had been friends with Giordano's girlfriend. It was the wife's testimony that Gary had asked his girlfriend to get a copy of her husband's signature.

In nearly four decades as a lawyer, Murphy said, "I've never seen anyone who had the gall to create, prepare and forge such a document."

The case nevertheless finally proceeded to trial in 2011. However, Giordano's hopes for a big win sunk like a stone on March 24, the day his girlfriend was scheduled to testify in court. However, she wasn't his girlfriend any longer; the couple had split more than a year earlier.

Giordano's lawyer filed to prevent her from testifying. This was the same woman who had accused Giordano of videotaping them having sex and then posting pornographic images of her on the Internet. This was the same woman who had filed a restraining order against Giordano, claiming he had told her that "the world would be a better place without" her, adding that "he could help." When the motion was denied by a judge, this was the woman who would be able to speak freely about him in open court. Giordano quickly dropped the case.

"I accused him of committing perjury, I accused him of fabricating documents, I accused him of the worst sort of behavior that I could think of," said Murphy. "My professional judgment about Mr. Giordano was that he was not to be believed at any level about anything."

Murphy would later appear on NBC's *Today Show*. When asked about Giordano, the attorney wasn't shy about his feelings. "He has the ability to create a lie, live the lie and try to make everyone else believe his lie." Murphy also cast further doubt on Giordano's story concerning Robyn's disappearance. "He (Giordano) doesn't go in a swimming pool. He doesn't go in the ocean because he wears a toupee and he doesn't get it wet."

≈ *19* ≈

Nearly two months had passed since Robyn Gardner vanished without a trace. "She would never give up on me, so I will do the same for her," Forester told one gossip website. "I feel like I would know deep down if she was dead."

Even though it admittedly sounded like denial, ex-boyfriend Richard Forester remained steadfast, tried keeping hope alive, to keep fighting.

Though no remains had been found, Aruban authorities had presumed Robyn dead weeks previous. Forester wasn't convinced. He told a reporter that he was making new friends through Twitter and Facebook and had been circulating "missing person" posters for Robyn that he had made himself. He also had contacted locals in Aruba and the surrounding Caribbean island.

Forester also divulged a shocking tidbit — many of the friendly Arubans he had been in contact with never followed the news and had barely even head of Robyn's story. "I just hope the authorities are doing everything they can," he said.

Forester's gut feeling led him to believe in the strong possibility that Giordano had an accomplice. "I don't think Gary is smart enough to do it by himself or he had enough time," said Forester. "Maybe she was removed from the island."

Whether she was still on the island or not, the search for clues remained centered on Aruba and the area around Baby Beach. In early October cadaver dogs were finally brought to the island from the Netherlands.

"I'm happy about it," said Forester. "I just wish they had done it sooner."

One person who agreed with Forester was Giordano's American attorney Jose Baez, calling it grossly unfair for cadaver dogs to have been brought in over two months after the fact. "Whatever scent of decomposition they expected to find is long gone."

After yet another release request was denied by a judge, Gary Giordano hired a second Aruban lawyer, this one from the Natalee Holloway case. Chris Lejuez had famously defended Nick John and Abraham Jones, two security guards who had been detained on suspicion of murdering and kidnapping Holloway. The guards, known for cruising hotels in search of female tourists, had somehow been implicated in statements made by main suspects Joran van der Sloot, Deepak Kalpoe, and his brother Satish. Eight days after their arrest, thanks to Lejeuz, suspects John and Jones were released without being charged.

Though Michael Lopez would remain on Giordano's Aruban defense team, it would be Lejuez who would take the reins. Lejuez reaffirmed the belief that the cops had nothing on his client. "They have tried all kinds of theories and strategies, and (Giordano's) story stands like a rock."

As the calendar wound down on October and Giordano sweltered in his stuffy cell, a photo began making the rounds. Aruban news sources had obtained a jailhouse surveillance camera image of Giordano after his toupee had been confiscated by authorities. Though the picture was grainy, Giordano, head slightly bowed, looked nothing like the Lothario depicted in the media. Instead, he appeared little more than a sad and frightened middle-aged male. If anything, the image of him without his hairpiece made him appear smaller than his 6'2", 210 pound frame.

Stress was definitely taking its toll on Giordano. Lejuez vehemently denied the reports that his client was again being uncooperative with the investigation.

"After you ask someone the same question six times, he may get frustrated when you ask him a seventh time," stated Lejuez. "They have been presenting him with different hypothesis, even with different witnesses, videos and photos, and he has still kept his story. Nothing has made him break it, contradict, or change it."

Giordano's sixty day sentence was drawing to a close and still no charges had been filed against him. Lejuez shifted his efforts into high gear.

Another closed door hearing was set for Friday October 28 to again determine if Gary Giordano would walk free.

It was August 5 that Giordano had been stopped at the airport just feet from boarding a plane back to the U.S. He had been covered in sweat. He told customs agents that his travel companion was taking another flight home.

He first had to deal with the vermin-infested cell of the San Nicolas police station jail where he had allegedly beat his fists against the wall and fought some kind of night terrors that brought on alleged cries of, "Robyn! I'm so sorry! Forgive me!" and "It's all my fault!"

Then came the hot box cell of KIA prison, a facility that overlooked the same southern tip of Aruba where Robyn Gardner had reportedly been swept out to sea. Days of interrogation passed where, according to local law, Giordano was not allowed to have a lawyer present even as he told and retold his rather eyebrow-raising story to investigators.

The police reenactment, the cadaver dogs, the searching volunteers combing the coastline — nothing so far had turned up a single clue tying Giordano to Robyn's disappearance. There was still not one shred of concrete evidence that pointed to a crime even having been committed.

October 28 arrived. The prosecution, desperate to keep their only suspect in custody, filed for one last extension. Cell phones, computers, and handwriting were still being examined. Most of that investigation was being done in labs off Aruba. Authorities begged for yet more time.

Giordano sat at the defense table. He appealed directly to the judge stating that he was clearly innocent. Lejuez argued that the prosecution had nothing on his client.

The defense's motion to allow Giordano's release was denied. Giordano would be held for up to thirty more days — but this would be their final extension.

"I am not confident that he will never be charged," Lejuez responded when later asked about his client. "But I am confident that if he is that I will have a lot of things to say about this case."

≈ 20 ≈

Psychic profiler Carla Baron not only believed Gary Giordano had something to do with Robyn Gardner's disappearance, she felt there was also something hinky about Richard Forrester.

Forester had appeared on dozens of TV news and talk shows; he had spoken to reporters around the world offering his hope that his girlfriend was somehow still alive. However, as the trail for clues in the investigation went cold, so did the media's interest. Three months after Robyn's disappearance, Forester launched a page for the Robyn Gardner Foundation on StayClassy.org, a website dedicated to helping nonprofit organizations build successful online fundraising initiatives.

While some met this charity initiative with sympathy and concern, others questioned whether Forrester's new charity was little more than a suspected cash grab. Questions surfaced over where the internet-solicited donations were going.

One major criticism levied against Forester was that he still had not traveled to Aruba to help search for Robyn or question authorities in person. Critics were also beginning to suggest that Forester himself was having money troubles.

Forester had been mired in legal proceedings against his ex-wife, Abbey, since their divorce in March of 2007. Things had been contentious between the former partners. Less than three weeks after the ink dried on the divorce decree, Abbey filed a domestic violence complaint against Forester which resulted in him being served with a protective order. Four days later, Forester filed to modify his child support and visitation. In the months to come, Abbey would drop the hammer by petitioning the court for enforcement of child support, medical bills and attorney's fees.

On December 2, 2010, ten months previous to Robyn's disappearance, the court ruled in Abbey's favor. A judgment for $103,705.83 was placed against Forester — a figure that included $19,000 in alimony, $43,318.83 for child support, $6,500 for unpaid activity fees, $2,568.72 health insurance reimbursement, $4,370.78 medical reimbursement, $1,512.50 for tutoring reimbursement, and $19,885 for attorney's fees, plus an additional $6,300 for the kids' college savings plan.

Forester lived in an modest apartment, not a $1.3 million house. The financial judgment against him was like the proverbial nail in Forester's financial coffin. If he wasn't using the funds in his charity to look for Robyn, flabbergasted critics cried, what was he doing with them?

Forester was losing the battle to be seen in a compassionate light. This was further muddied by accusations of cyber-bullying his critics on Facebook. Social conversation about Robyn's story was being tainted by the lack of sympathy Forester received from those who believed his behavior indicated hidden skeletons in his own closet. Even his declarations that all donations to the Robyn Gardner Foundation were tax-deductible were coming under fire. Forester claimed that the charity had filed for tax-exempt status, but had not yet been approved; his statements were falling on deaf ears. Ultimately nothing substantive could be achieved by the foundation because not enough money had been raised.

Heading Forester's list of public foes, psychic Carla Baron continued to rail against Robyn Gardner's former boyfriend. Forester had initially contacted Baron back on August 12, ten days after Robyn had vanished. Though he had asked for help, things quickly went sour between them. Two weeks later, Baron blogged about dissolving her association with the case because of "a certain individual in the news at present," remarking that "he has treated me with no respect for my well-known intuitive abilities, & what I have given — 'pro bono' throughout — toward his search and resolution to find Robyn Gardner, bringing those guilty to justice."

Baron would later post more details as to her brief association with that "certain individual:" Richard Forester.

I had asked Richard many times if we could please concentrate on the crime details with Robyn's disappearance, and see what specifically I could get on Gary Giordano's direct involvement. But Richard avoided this topic like the plague.

All Richard wanted to do was see if I could 'talk' to Robyn, and "Where was she now? Was she right beside him? Would she get into bed with him? Was she riding in the car next to him?"

Also:

Richard Forester had the "hot one minute/ cold the next" temperament I have found in other predators' behavior. Still present, but to a lesser degree. Not in the sinister vein which can turn criminal. This could have been why Robyn Gardner was attracted to him in this relationship… then perhaps having second thoughts as time went on with Richard.

In her lengthy diatribe, Baron went on to say that she had received many unsolicited emails from those who claimed to know Forester. Most of the stories they told were unfavorable, bathing Forester in a much different light than his public persona of the grieving boyfriend back home.

The allegations made by Baron against Forester were indeed volatile, though perhaps none more explosive than the following posted on her site:

A last text received by Christina Jones from Robyn Gardner in Aruba revealed she was BREAKING UP w/ Richard Forester upon her return.

≈ *21* ≈

Gabe Watson had lost his wife and now he was facing the grim prospect of spending the rest of his life behind bars. For years Tina Thomas's father had been pushing Australian authorities to bring Gabe to trial for her murder. Relations between Gabe and Tina's parents had never been rosy even during their engagement; after Tina died things between them deteriorated from bad to untenable.

In 2005, Gabe had Tina's body exhumed and moved to his family's Birmingham cemetery plot. He had taken possession of her Jeep, clothes, furniture, and wedding gifts: basically everything she owned. When her parents pleaded for him to return her school and college yearbooks, Gabe turned them away.

He certainly wasn't going to allow Tina's body to be moved back into her original grave.

Tommy and Cindy Thomas had placed a vase with flowers at Tina's new grave. They were so certain Gabe would throw it away that they chained the vase in to her headstone with a bicycle lock.

That didn't deter Gabe. He used a pair of bolt cutters to remove the chain and discard the plastic flowers. When Tina's parents suspected their former son-in-law of desecrating the gifts they left at their daughter's grave, they got local police to set up a hidden camera sting until they were able to catch Gabe in the act.

Obviously guilty of vandalizing his wife's grave, Gabe explained that Tina loved fresh flowers and would have hated the plastic ones her parents left. With no other way to remove them, he was forced to use cutters.

It also didn't seem to help matters that Gabe had remarried. The fact that he had moved on with his life left a very bitter taste into the mouths of his former in-laws.

"You never think your daughter will leave for her honeymoon and her husband will kill her," Cindy Thomas told ABC News.

Gabe convicted and sentenced for murder in an Australian court would be the justice they had been looking for in the name of the daughter who had been taken away too early.

So they thought.

In order to avoid a trial, Queensland prosecutors allowed Gabe to cop to manslaughter instead of murder. Gabe's plea bargain would have him admit guilt to an obscure Australian law that states if you undertake a risky activity with someone, you have a greater responsibility of ensuring their safety.

Essentially, Gabe Watson was pleading guilty to failure to save his dive buddy.

The Prosecutor asked for six years behind bars at the Borallon Correctional Centre. Watson's own lawyer felt the best his client could do was a four year term, with parole after sixteen months.

Justice Peter Lyons of Supreme Court at Brisbane delivered the sentence to Gabe and shocked the world.

"Stand up, please, Mr. Watson. You stand convicted on your plea of guilty of the offense of manslaughter causing the death of your wife. The offense occurred when you had both been diving in the vicinity of the historical shipwreck *Yongala* some 48 nautical miles east of Townsville.

"An offense such as manslaughter which involves the loss of a human life is obviously a very serious matter. The deceased was 26 years old. You were recently married. She had every reason to look forward to a long and happy life. Her death is also a great tragedy for her family. I have read the victim impact statements. They demonstrate that she and her family were very close and that she was very close to her friend. They demonstrate how deeply her loss is felt by all of them. Her family, obviously and naturally, take a very serious view of your conduct and that, not surprisingly, appears in their statements.

"You have voluntarily returned from the United States and have surrendered yourself into custody in Australia. In my view, it is quite significant that at the time of your return you did not know that the Crown would not persist in charging you with murder, which carries a mandatory sentence of life imprisonment. You no doubt expected that you would be sentenced to a term of imprisonment for a substantial period in what for you is a foreign country. You have, in fact, acknowledged that you are guilty of manslaughter. You do not seek to pretend that your actions were other than what they were. In doing so, you have spared the deceased's family the agony of a trial.

"You have provided a number of references from people who appear to be quite reputable and to know you well. They confirm that you are of good character. They also reveal that you are a person who is known to help others and that you loved your wife and were devastated by her loss.

"There have been, in some of your statements, some inconsistencies and some attempts to put blame on other people. There does not seem to be any persistence in your attempt to put blame on anyone else and you accept that the responsibility for this loss is yours alone. The inconsistencies and those attempts, to me, while they do not speak particularly well of you, should be looked at in the circumstances in which they occurred. That is, they occurred shortly after the dive and at a time when you, no doubt, were deeply upset by the events which have occurred.

"The seriousness of the matter, notwithstanding the factors which I take into account in mitigation, means that it is necessary to impose a penalty which provides for a substantial period of imprisonment. I therefore propose to impose a head sentence of four and a half years.

"Because of the mitigating factors which I have identified and because I accept that for you in Australia time in prison will be harder than it will be for people who serve a sentence of imprisonment in their own country, I intend to fix a suspension date a little earlier than might otherwise have been the case.

"I order that the term of imprisonment be suspended after a period of 12 months' imprisonment."

Tina's parents were stunned. After pleading guilty to not doing enough to save their daughter's life, Gabe was going to walk in just one year.

≈ *22* ≈

In October 2011, *The National Enquirer* went public with an unsubstantiated rumor that Giordano had taped a plastic bag over Robyn's head and buried her alive. A source told the magazine that the Maryland businessman had driven to Dog's Grave Beach and dug up a fresh grave with his hands, removed a dog's corpse, widened the hole and put Robyn in it. He then allegedly put the dead dog's body on top of hers with her moaning and moving as he filled up the hole.

One month later, Aruban attorney Michael Lopez formally stepped down as Giordano's mouthpiece. Though he was no longer representing the accused, Lopez steadfastly stood by his former client's innocence. "There is no proof whatsoever that Mr. Giordano has committed an offense. Mr. Giordano soon will have to be released," he told reporters.

Chris Lejuez was now Giordano's head Aruban counsel. "I am not confident that he will never been charged," Lejuez had stated. While it didn't appear to be a rousing endorsement of his client, Lejuez was dealing with a slight language barrier. Though his command of English was a bit weak, his confidence in his client's chances of going free was not.

Nothing had changed in the police investigation. Authorities continued to scramble to piece together a case against Giordano. Some even wondered if Giordano — a trained tech expert with a degree in Computer Sciences — was capable of wiping away any electronic traces of a crime.

Authorities had to hope that keeping Giordano behind bars for another thirty days would be enough time for them to find the elusive link between his seemingly suspicious behavior, the perceived inconsistency of his statements, and his sweat-soaked fumbling mannerisms in front of airport customs officers as he tried to explain that the travel companion he had entered the country with was going to be taking another flight.

The elusive link didn't surface in time. The deadline for release was upon them.

Giordano and lawyer Chris Lejeuz expected another attempt to extend Giordano's imprisonment on November 25. The defense team was given quite a shock.

The judge instead ordered Giordano released from prison.

Aruban Solicitor General Taco Stein immediately filed to appeal the order, calling Giordano a "suspect in a suspicious death."

Conceding that there was merit, the judge agreed to hear the prosecution's final appeal the following Monday. If Taco's motion was denied, Giordano would be free to leave the country.

Giordano still wasn't celebrating, despite seeing light at the end of his incarceration tunnel. Lejuez told reporters that his client was still very concerned, and would "only feel relieved once he was on a plane back home." Lejeuz added, in typical lawyerese: "Once he is free, he can do as he pleases. I am very happy for him."

That fateful Monday November 28, Taco Stein's last ditch legal maneuver was denied. The judge ruled that authorities couldn't justify keeping Giordano locked up. The following evening, the only suspect police had in the disappearance of Robyn Gardner was released after 116 days in jail. Gary Giordano was a free man.

There was no body. No physical evidence. No elusive link.

Donning a baseball cap in place of his iconic toupee, Giordano left the prison as curious onlookers blocked his car to catch a glimpse at the supposed "monster" in the flesh. Taunts of "murderer!" greeted Giordano at his hotel. Once in his suite, much larger than the bathroom-sized stuffy cell he had shared with two other inmates, the first thing Giordano did was make an emotional phone call home to his three sons.

"I'm relieved for him," said Jose Baez, Giordano's American lawyer who had choreographed his client's defense from the sidelines. "A great injustice has been done."

Now Giordano's scramble to get out of Aruba was on.

≈ *23* ≈

Come morning, Taco Stein would try yet again to ask the court to detain Gary Giordano. He was preparing an extradition request back to Aruba if he could find a way to charge his only suspect.

"We know he has been lying about what happened," said Taco. "His description of the situation is not in accordance with reality." Taco was not buying "storm" theory that Giordano had given as the cause for the strong current. Taco claimed that the weather that day was calm with no wind.

But Taco Stein still had no actual proof. All he had in hand was a mountain of circumstantial evidence.

"It's time for them to cut bait," Baez replied when told of the prosecution's intentions. He described his client as a man who has had his life, reputation, and business destroyed in the wake of Taco Stein's "fishing expedition."

Giordano had no intention of lingering on the island. He had a ticket for a morning flight that was scheduled to go wheels up before Stein's next hearing.

A tsunami of outcry against Giordano's release came from across the world; many were stunned by the very eerie similarity to the case of Natalee Holloway just six years earlier. The entire Aruban justice system that couldn't assemble a case against suspect Joran van der Sloot had been globally criticized as a bumbling bunch of Keystone Cops. Now they had failed again.

There were others, however, yet unheard, who actually had a pressing motive to get Giordano off the island - Aruba's official number one industry: tourism.

The small nation could ill afford to go into the lucrative winter vacation season with another high-profile criminal case dominating international headlines. Even though Joran van der Sloot had subsequently murdered 21 year old Stephany Flores in a Peru hotel room, whatever had been done was no longer Aruba's problem.

Though Taco Stein vowed investigators wouldn't rest until they unearthed the truth about what really happened to Robyn Gardner, those familiar with the machinations of the American justice system weren't optimistic. There was almost zero chance the U.S. would grant extradition unless Aruba had enough concrete evidence to bring murder charges against Giordano.

Robyn's ex-boyfriend Richard Forester was not pleased, nor was he surprised Giordano had been released from custody. While Giordano relaxed aboard a flight headed back to the U.S., an online gossip reporter reached Forester. "What I'm really not happy about is we still don't know where Robyn is," he replied. He was angry at Aruban authorities for spending four months trying to build a case against Giordano — and ultimately failing — instead of using more resources to find Robyn.

"What happened to the witness? What happened to the blood that was on the towel? What happened to the rental car that was seen in the video?" he inquired.

Even worse for Forrester was knowing that Giordano would be returning to the $1.3 million mansion that was located a scant ten minutes away from the Bethesda apartment Forester had shared with Robyn. Forester admitted he was unsure what he would do if he ran into Giordano locally. He added that at the least he would be compelled, not to violence against the last man to see Robyn alive, but to instead confront Giordano about where Robyn was, what he did with her and why he would lie about them snorkeling.

"He's not a well-liked man and there's a lot of people out there," claimed Forester. He also pointed that he would be actually heartbroken if his nemesis were to somehow end up dead; with Giordano gone, all of his secrets would vanish with him, including the best chance of ever knowing the truth.

$$\approx 24 \approx$$

Two days after landing back on American soil, a toupee-clad Giordano opened up to NBC's *Dateline* in a televised interview. In front of a camera, he told the story of what happened that day.

"We drifted out. And then I noticed that the — we were getting in deeper water. So I reached out to grab her leg, pulled her leg to signal going in. And as I turned, my shoes had become extremely heavy, cause we were being pushed out by the wind and some current. And now I was struggling. So that's the last time I saw her. That's the last image I have of her," claimed Giordano. He further reiterated the water had gotten rough.

"It was and I told them that it — at a certain point, I was struggling to get back. So you can determine what rough is, you know. There wasn't a tidal wave coming at me, but I was struggling — at one point I realized this is — there's a problem here."

When confronted about his apparent casual manner seen on the surveillance tape which showed him knocking on the windows of the bar moments after he had gotten out of the water, Giordano claimed it looked that way because he was: "exhausted, scared and shocked there was nobody there."

Much like Gabe Watson, Gary Giordano conceded that the alleged motive of insurance was the key factor in his accusal. Had he not bought the Amex travel coverage for Robyn, he would not have been held.

As Giordano continued his post-release television media tour, he began to float his own new theory about Robyn's disappearance.

"Aruba has two main sources of income and it's not from tourism. It's cocaine and human trafficking," Giordano told ABC's *Good Morning America.*

The specter of human trafficking in Aruba had raised its unspeakable head before during the Natalee Holloway investigation. Prime suspect Joran van der Sloot even later admitted during a sit-down interview on Fox TV that he had *sold* Natalee to a Venezuelan man for $10,000!

According to van der Sloot, a notorious partier when he lived on Aruba, he had met a Venezuelan man in a casino. The man, somewhere between 30 and 40, offered Joran $10,000 cash if he could "bring him a blonde girl." Sometime later, after spotting a very drunk Holloway at Carlos n' Charlies nightclub, van der Sloot managed to separate her from her friends. He called a number the man had given him and was given a location: Marriott Beach.

There, van der Sloot said, he watched as a boat pulled up around 1:30 a.m. The man from the casino handed him a paper bag with cash inside. The man took Holloway by the hand and escorted the unsuspecting girl onto the boat. She didn't even struggle as the boat quickly motored into the cloak of darkness.

Many non-believers who had seen the interview dismissed van der Sloot's claims as yet more perverse and wild tales being spun by a pathological liar. However, van der Sloot's story took a more sinister turn that would send a chill up the spine of even the most hardened skeptic.

When authorities in Aruba were unable to fashion a case against him in Holloway's suspicious disappearance, van der Sloot returned home to Holland. Once there, he got involved in a scheme to bring girls from Thailand into the country so they could each be sold to a Dutch prostitution ring for $13,000 cash. After lying to his parents that he wanted to move to Bangkok to finish school, van der Sloot enrolled in Rangsit University, but only as a cover. At night, he would assume a fake identity as a recruiter in charge of finding young exotic dancers from Thailand for high-paid gigs in Holland — gigs that of course didn't exist.

It was this very activity that van der Sloot was up to in 2008 when he was caught on hidden camera by Dutch investigative journalist Peter R. De Vries. Recorded on tape, van der Sloot can be seen in a hotel room full of underage girls offering them "$15,000 to shake your ass."

Dutch authorities began a half-hearted investigation into van der Sloot's alleged activities, but never brought charges. In 2010, van der Sloot would murder 21 year old Stephany Flores in a Peru hotel room.

Two months earlier, van der Sloot had attempted to extort $250,000 from Natalee Holloway's family by promising to reveal more about what happened to her.

In January, 2012 van der Sloot pleaded guilty to the "qualified murder" and robbery of Flores. He was sentenced to 28 years behind bars, where he remains today.

Though it may seem van der Sloot's psychopathic disregard for others had seen its share of victims, there was one last revelation that chillingly echoed back to his once-outrageous claim that he had sold Natalee Holloway into the sex trade.

Two of the young Thai girls who are seen with him in that hidden camera hotel room video have gone missing.

Human trafficking in Aruba is not just the nightmarish stuff of urban myth. It absolutely exists. In 2008, the same year Dutch journalist Peter R. De Vries recorded his infamous van der Sloot video, two men — 36 year old Venezuelan Hector Acosta and 44 year old Columbian Henry Gonzalez Henao — were arrested when the Aruban Coast Guard detected their small boat on radar as it was making suspicious movements.

When the craft was boarded, it was running without lights and without registration. Eighteen other "passengers" were on board. Both men were convicted for being involved in human trafficking and sentenced to prison.

In fact, a report issued by the United Nations in 2012 admits that Aruba is a destination for women subjected to sex trafficking and forced labor. It also mentions that there are clear indications of children under the age of 18 that are exploited through prostitution on Aruba.

It also cannot be dismissed that the next closest body of land to this tiny island country is Venezuela, a notorious haven not just for drugs, but also for human trafficking of girls sold into the sex trade. A scant seventeen miles away from Aruba, Venezuela is a mere half hour trip by boat.

Not everyone bought Gary Giordano's suspicion of human trafficking, but one person who wasn't dismissing it was ex-boyfriend Richard Forester. On a TV interview taped shortly after Giordano's appearance, Forester said that this very subject had been something he feared as a possibility from the beginning. If so, he surmised that Giordano still could have been involved. "There's a whole underworld down there," said Forester. "I don't know what he knows about Aruba."

Forester wasn't the only one who openly suspected Giordano could have been involved in some type of scheme to sell Robyn into the sex trade. All sorts of wild theories had begun to pop up on the Internet, many suggesting that Giordano had done it because of his financial troubles. Some even believed that Giordano's Italian name implied that he was in some way hooked up with *La Cosa Nostra*, the American Mafia.

Forester himself was not without his own detractors, who suspected he was not quite the loving boyfriend he pretended to be. Psychic Carla Baron offered another shocking, yet unverified inference that a broken arm Robyn had suffered months before her disappearance had been caused by Forester. Some internet theorists went so far as to suggest that Forester and Giordano were somehow in it together because they both had money problems.

Then there was the alleged mystery man who had been seen talking to Robyn at the Rum Reef Bar & Grill for ten minutes on the day she vanished. The tattooed 40-ish white American had left the bar shortly after Giordano and Robyn. Authorities were never able to identify him.

Reunited with his three sons back home, Giordano continued to be vilified by those who felt he didn't seem emotional enough over the loss, and apparent death, of his (girl) friend Robyn Gardner. Giordano attempted to counter his critics by going on TV and claiming that he still hadn't come to grips with what had happened. Oddly enough, when asked about Robyn, Giordano commented "I personally feel like I'll see her again."

Forester's own offensive against Giordano came to a bitter standoff during Geraldo Rivera's TV show when lawyer Jose Baez warned Forester that he was "walking a fine line in terms of a defamation suit."

"Baez was trying to bully me," said Forester later. "I don't get bullied."

It was during that same Geraldo interview that Giordano agreed it would be "accurate" to describe Robyn Gardner as promiscuous.

While not defending Robyn's reputation, Giordano certainly chose to fight misconceptions about himself with more TV appearances. On *Good Morning America,* he was asked directly about why he would take out that kind of insurance policy on a companion in a casual relationship. With Jose Baez by his side, Giordano explained "I've purchased it many times before, it's cancellation insurance, it's travel insurance. The first thing is cancellation insurance and when you click that button you have to enter the names, if we were traveling the three of us, I could type in the three names, or just your name. But then when you go further down and click the medical and the emergency dental, and the accident insurance, when you select those, if I put three names up there, all three are covered. You can't unselect anybody. So I maxed out on everything. Medical, I think was $150,000, but that's automatic, I can't unselect Robyn. And when it came down to the accident insurance, you can't unselect her. So when I was selecting that, I was selecting it for me and she got the same thing."

By purchasing cancellation coverage for Robyn's ticket, Giordano claimed he was forced to add her to all of the extra coverages he was purchasing for himself, including accidental death.

From the beginning, Giordano had been publicly eviscerated for contacting Amex about the travel insurance so soon after Robyn had vanished. He explained that his first Aruban attorney, Michael Lopez, told him to make the call. The search and rescue boats and helicopters the authorities were planning on using were all privately owned and he could potentially be handed an invoice for their time and services.

According to Jose Baez, however, Lopez may have had ulterior motives of his own and an eye on dollar signs. At the time Giordano hadn't realized that Lopez was also a personal injury lawyer on the island. It wasn't until Giordano was asked to sign a retainer agreement to give Lopez one third of any insurance monies collected that a huge conflict of interest was discovered.

"If you're in a foreign country, and you don't know how things operate there, and trust me when you're in a completely different land, the language is different, the culture is different. Your rights are different. You're going to follow what you think is sound advice. And if your lawyer is telling you something, I don't think anyone would argue with following their lawyer's advice," said Baez.

If anything, Lopez was going down the checklist given in a government travel advisory. According to Giordano, a handbook produced by the Dutch government states that in case of a missing person the first call to make is to authorities and the second is to your insurance company.

≈ *25* ≈

Despite the public outcry over the leniency of Gabe Watson's sentence, the man now known around the world as "The Honeymoon Killer" would only serve a total of eighteen months before being released from prison. Prosecutors appealed to keep him in jail longer, but the appellate panel agreed that Gabe had not originally plead guilty to any intentional inflicting of harm, nor was he sentenced on the basis of any malevolent intent.

Upon his release, Gabe was deported back to the United States to face capitol murder charges being brought against him in the state of Alabama. Belief that Gabe had planned to kill Tina while back home before the wedding gave prosecutors confidence that they had jurisdiction to press charges. Troy King, then Alabama's Attorney General, bought into the theory that insurance had been the motive.

In February of 2012, with TV crews from all over the world watching, the trial of Gabe Watson for the kidnapping and murder of Tina Watson began in the Jefferson County Criminal Courts in Birmingham, Alabama. However, after only eight days of witness testimony, it was clear the state was not going to overcome the hurdles of circumstantial evidence and reasonable doubt. Gabe's lawyer filed a motion to dismiss with a judgment for acquittal.

The claim that Gabe killed his wife for financial gain remained unproven. Tina's liabilities greatly outweighed her $3,000 in assets. As it turned out, Tina had never increased her insurance policy, nor had she changed the beneficiary from her father to her husband — a fact that Gabe hadn't discovered until after her death.

The only financial claim made by Gabe at all was $10,000 against his travel insurance to cover the cost of bringing Tina's body home. Morosely, he had joked with the agent that if he had bought more insurance, he would have still been in jail in Australia.

Presiding Judge Tommy Nail agreed with Gabe's attorneys. The case was dismissed. Gabe Watson was acquitted of the murder of his wife.

While Tina Watson's death was very tragic, and despite public outcry for Gabe to be held accountable for her murder, all the evidence gathered by courts in two separate countries indicated otherwise.

Perhaps Judge Chesterman of the Supreme Court of Queensland Court of Appeal said it best.

"I think likely that the respondent (Gabe) left his wife because when confronted with a novel, difficult and dangerous situation he lacked the qualities of character, and the skills, to deal with it... The respondent was wrongly accused in the public eye of murder."

Doctor Carl Edmonds, one of the world's most esteemed specialists in the field of diving and subaquatic medicine, studied the evidence in the Tina Watson case extensively. He came to the following conclusions:

Tina Watson suffered the two commonest causes of death in young scuba divers, drowning and pulmonary barotrauma.

She had most of the contributing causes for these. She was medically, physically and psychologically unsuited for the dive she undertook. She was inexperienced, doing the deepest dive she had ever attempted, her first dive in open water and against currents she had never encountered previously She was over-weighted and without adequate supervision.

She panicked, was probably exhausted and over-breathed her regulator, aspirated water, became hypoxic, lost consciousness and, finally, drowned. This was complicated by bursting her lungs during a rapid emergency ascent.

How anyone could claim that there was no reason for her death, or attribute it to a murder, is beyond my comprehension.

Gabe would tell a national TV audience that he didn't know that Tina had never been in the ocean before. He claimed he didn't know a "red flag" dive was for advanced divers. He claimed he didn't know the Great Barrier Reef was fraught with sharks and strong currents.

"We're on vacation. They're going to be nice, easy, pretty dives," he claimed.

≈ *26* ≈

There's a story I first wrote about in the first *Fatal Sunset* book "Deadly Vacations."

In March of 1999, 39 year-old Mark Monazzami, an Iranian-born computer engineer from Sunnyvale, California, arrived in Maui for a belated honeymoon with his bride, 29 year-old Nahid Davoobadabi. Like many West Maui visitors, they rented a kayak to explore the shoreline.

The trip would end in disaster.

The seas were calm. Monazzami and Davoobadabi stayed close to the beach but unexpectedly strong winds kicked up, blowing the pair far from shore. Before they knew it, Monazzami and his wife were in over their heads, literally, as the gusting squalls capsized their kayak several times while they struggled to get back to land. By nightfall, the current had taken the heavily-fatigued pair deep into the channel between Maui and neighboring Molokai. They clung desperately to the overturned kayak, trying to stay out of the chilling wind.

When danger struck, it came quickly. "Shark!" shouted Davoobadabi just before being pulled under. In moments, the ocean was red. Her arm was missing, bitten off. Monazzami tried to pull her aboard the kayak. Unable to control the bleeding, he could only cradle her as she died. Buffeted by strong winds in the rough seas, he was unable to hold onto her. Sometime during the night, her body slipped into the water and vanished.

Drifting on the kayak overnight, Monozzami made it to the rocky shore of Kaho'olawe, an uninhabited island owned by the government and used for munitions testing. After wandering for two days, Monozzami came across an old military bunker. Inside, by some small miracle, was a working telephone.

After being airlifted back to Maui, he recounted his tale to authorities who listed the incident as an unconfirmed shark attack. Davoobadabi's body was never recovered and some who doubt Monozzami's tale have speculated that he may have instead murdered his wife.

But speculation without fact is not evidence.

Slated to testify for the defense in Alabama's case against Gabe Watson was Michael McFayden, a scuba expert with several thousand hours of dive time. McFayden calculated that it was the amount of air left in Tina Watson's scuba tank that proved that Gabe could not have killed her in the manner specifically described by prosecutors.

Both Tina and Gabe's dive computers were similar to airplane black boxes, logging each diver's depth, mapped over time. From the data, we know it took the couple three and a half minutes to descend to a depth around fifteen meters. Some two minutes later, Tina's body began to sink down to the ocean floor while Gabe started a quick ascent to the surface.

Medically speaking, it takes a minimum of two minutes of oxygen deprivation — more likely three minutes or more — to kill someone. This means Gabe would have had to shut off her air sometime around the three minute mark of their dive.

Gabe then allegedly turned the air tank back on after she was dead to conceal the crime and then let her body sink to the bottom. If this had been the case, any subsequent air usage would have been incidental. All of Tina's dive gear was found completely functional with her body. There was nothing wrong with her air tanks or her hoses or mouthpiece.

Given the amount of air that was left in her tank, if Tina had only been alive for the first three minutes of her dive she would have needed to consume a physically impossible amount of oxygen during that time. A normal scuba diver will use an average of 28 liters of air per minute during a slow, steady swim. A panicked diver can consume 60-70 liters per minute. Tina's air consumption would have needed to average 100 liters per minute for three full minutes if she had perished immediately after. A human just cannot breathe that much air.

There is just no way her air could have been turned off. The amount of air left in Tina's tank more accurately fits a model that shows an increasing amount of air being used over time as her panicked breathing fatally led to her drowning death around the six minute mark of the dive.

In the case of Gabe's dive computer battery issues it should be noted that electronic devices of this nature that retain information require extremely low levels of power to keep data stored in memory. Oceanic, the device's manufacturer, suggests taking the batteries out of the unit if you aren't planning to use the dive computer for a week. When turned back on, even with the batteries placed backwards in the compartment, there is enough juice in the unit to power the battery warning light. By the time investigators had inspected the unit, the capacitors that stored this tiny bit of backup power had completely discharged, rendering the unit dead.

To better understand why all of this data had not been interpreted correctly by authorities, one must look no further than a detective team that lacked proper dive knowledge or McFaydens' level of experience, or the botched reenactment run by local police divers who were used to working in shallower waters close to shore. They had never investigated a case like this, in conditions such as those at the Great Barrier Reef.

Inescapable is the fact that Tina Watson had been medically, physically and psychologically unsuited for this dive. She was inexperienced, carrying too much extra dive weight, and was without adequate supervision.

According to Dr. Carl Edmonds, the world's leading specialist for dive medicine, "She panicked, was probably exhausted and over-breathed her regulator, aspirated water, became hypoxic, lost consciousness and, finally, drowned."

And then there was Gabe. Not only had he wrongly misjudged his qualifications as experience, but he had fatally mistaken Tina's handful of dives in a shallow pool at an Alabama quarry as adequate preparation for their adventures.

Was this crusade against Gabe Watson, as well as his very public crucifixion, the product of a human nature that strongly desires having a villain to blame for the bad things that happen?

Rather than believe someone we care about could make a fatal misjudgment about the elements of nature they were about to enter — that they were just in the wrong place at the wrong time, ultimately making an unalterable choice — the human mind prefers to find fault with a real person rather than to throw blame at the random and seemingly senseless cruelty of Mother Nature.

Is it so difficult for us, as people, to reconcile that the villain sometimes really is Mother Nature herself? That bad things actually can happen to good people?

Diving had been *Gabe's* hobby. Tina had learned in order to please him. She had suffered from panicked breathing while on her beginning dives in the still waters of an Alabama quarry. She did not have the requisite skills or experience to dive the

Great Barrier Reef because she hadn't been trained in appropriate conditions for the trip. In addition, the *Spoilsport's* divemaster had not enforced Australian law which would have prohibited a diver with so little experience to get into the water without proper supervision.

Compounding everything was Gabe's panicked reaction, though it's uncertain if any attempts to swim after his rapidly sinking wife would not have doomed him to a watery death as well.

It's easy to believe in your heart that you would "die trying" if ever faced with the unthinkable task of having to save a family member's life. However, if you have never been such a position, how could you really know for sure? Categorize Gabe Watson as a coward if you will, or someone of less-than-stellar character, but you cannot ignore that there is preponderance of evidence to support that he did not murder his wife.

But is he responsible?

In May of 2012, Gary Giordano was arrested for indecent exposure in the state of Maryland. Police discovered him naked in the back of his Escalade in a public parking garage, while having sex with 45 year-old Carol Ann Bock of Springfield, Tennessee.

By June, Giordano was suing Amex for $3.5 million. Two months later, the Amex Assurance Company, an American Express subsidiary, filed a countersuit. They claimed that the policy he purchased wasn't legally enforceable because Giordano and Gardner weren't married or otherwise related, weren't business partners, and didn't own property together. Amex Assurance's suit also accused Giordano of lying on insurance forms when he identified Robyn as his "partner" when, in truth, the pair were in a relationship that Amex described as "casual and non-exclusive."

Maryland criminal attorney, former prosecutor, and occasional legal commentator Rene Sandler categorized Gary Giordano's past as "a pattern of schemes and fraud, and just scams on other people." She agreed with one local radio personality's assessment of Giordano as a "con artist" and someone capable of "statements that don't make any sense at all."

Sandler explained "I reviewed the court records and files prior to that interview which revealed a pattern of theft allegations which included a conviction for a theft scheme. Theft scheme in Maryland involves a continuing course of conduct involving deception/intent to do same upon victim. My comments are consistent with his record, types of charges filed against him and elements of those offenses, and media reports from interviews of those who knew Giordano as well as my experience as a former prosecutor here in Montgomery County, Maryland and as a defense attorney for the past fifteen years."

Giordano wasn't exactly making tons of friends back home. A couple months earlier, he had been thrown out and permanently banned from Clyde's, a local bar in Rockville, Maryland for being drunk and obnoxious. Clyde's had also been a regular hangout for Richard Forester and Robyn Gardner. Giordano's sudden frequenting of the place, along with talking about prison and allegedly never showing remorse or sadness for Robyn, had rubbed some patrons and staff the wrong way.

For certain, one thing that stirred up public suspicion of Giordano was that Robyn's then-boyfriend Richard Forester claimed she never would have gone snorkeling because of her hair extensions and makeup.

After over two years together, he would have to be in a position to know, right?

How, then, is it possible that Forester had zero idea Robyn was meeting up with Giordano and going away with him to another country? What else did he *not* know about her?

Perhaps, caught up in emotional turmoil with Forester, being recently unemployed, and mired in an alimony battle with ex-husband Kenneth Gardner, Robyn simply chose to throw all of her inhibitions to the wind as an escape from it all.

Those "pornographic" photos found on Giordano's camera, the existence of which was later confirmed by Jose Baez, never really materialized into anything more than dirty pictures taken between two consenting adults. Robyn was an aspiring model at an age far past when most successful models have retired. Model Mayhem, the site where she had listed herself, has been not-so-kindly described as a place "where models go that are less than 3rd rate or also do porn/soft & hard." Robyn had also put up a profile at a reality show casting site. (As of this writing, both of these profiles are still online, though not terribly easy to find.)

If one is to believe tainted character witness Carrie Emerson's story about Giordano's interest in taking her daughter on a modeling shoot in Aruba, could his playing some sort of "Svengali" during a vulnerable time in Robyn's life compel her to do something she would not normally do?

Is that more plausible than the idea that Giordano had somehow done to Robyn what prosecutors in Australia and Alabama suspected Gabe Watson had done to his wife Tina? Could it be that Robyn and Giordano were drunk, alone on Baby Beach, and decided to have sex in the water and something went wrong?

Who's to say she didn't just see the crystal clear blue waters of Aruba teeming with tropical fish and figured it may be interesting to try? As the saying goes: "when in Rome…"

Perhaps being a little (or a lot) drunk, and maybe a bit groggy from the sleeping pill she had taken only hours before — regardless of how those intoxicants made it into her body — could have affected her inhibitions, judgment, ability to identify a dangerous situation, and ultimately, her ability to get herself out of trouble.

Forester's suspicion that Robyn would never go snorkeling was due to his suspicion that her hair extensions would come off in the water. In that same regard, I wondered if it was even possible for Giordano to go snorkeling with a toupee.

Apparently there are very strong adhesive tapes used to affix a wig to a scalp so it can be safely worn in water as well as methods of attaching hair extensions that don't dissolve in the ocean.

On the Rum Reef surveillance tape, taken during the moments when Giordano claimed he was trying to get someone's attention to call for help, he can clearly be seen wearing his rug. The toupee's appearance itself is no smoking gun.

I have read everything about this story. I want to believe he's guilty. When it comes to Robyn Gardner, there is one main reason why, in the absence of any new evidence, a case against Gary Giordano makes no sense to any prosecutor.

Reasonable doubt.

You can call him a pervy weirdo in a bad toupee. You can say that the trail of his past indiscretions is proof that he is not a person who most would consider as someone of sparkling character.

When describing what happened out in the water on that fateful day, Giordano recalled "My focus is on me... and I'm thinking that she'll find her way back. Did I yell for her, I don't think so... How can I help her when I need help?"

You can say, in the spirit of Gabe Watson's Australian conviction, that Giordano was guilty of being a bad swim buddy.

As the same reasonable and intelligent society that is able to initiate the judicial concept of "innocent until proven guilty," are we able to ask ourselves whether it is possible that Gary Giordano *did not* murder Robyn Gardner?

≈ *28* ≈

It is hard not to wonder if Gary Giordano is somehow responsible for Robyn Gardner's fate.

Or to wonder if there's anything else he may know that he hasn't told anyone.

Due to the eerie similarities between the strange disappearances of Robyn Gardner and Natalee Holloway, Giordano will always share an unsavory association with psychopathic confessed killer Joran van der Sloot. Though Joran van der Sloot's story continued to shift and change, Giordano's was consistent though vague. Giordano's larcenous past and his obviously fringe lifestyle didn't help paint a flattering portrait of him either. He is definitely guilty of referring to Robyn Gardner as a playmate rather than a lover. He dehumanized her into a sexual plaything whose loss was a great inconvenience to him.

Part of me wants to believe that the dark cloud of negative attention hanging over Gary Giordano is some kind of karmic retribution for all those things he had perpetrated before. But to believe that is akin to believing we all get what we deserve.

Tina Watson definitely did not get what *she* deserved.

Was she was guilty of allegedly marrying Gabe because the age of 30 was looking lonely without the addition of "Mr. Right Now?" Or of manufacturing enthusiasm to learn how to scuba dive only to appease the man her parents hated? Certainly she was guilty of underestimating the dangerous situation she was putting herself into by going on an advanced dive without the proper skills, experience or supervision.

Robyn Gardner did not get what *she* deserved.

Was she guilty of being someone who wanted a little more out of life?

It's very sad to think there will never be answers to the questions about what ultimately happened to Robyn. It is not murder. It's nature. It's not about guilt. It's about this ugly truth that *danger exists everywhere*. Going on vacation and casting away the worrier's mindset does not free you from your responsibility to look out for your own personal safety. Life is not some poker match where you can ask to be dealt out of a few hands while you go for a smoke. Life is going to keep you in the game and those bad cards could still come when you least expect.

In our hearts and minds, we desire to envision nature as being pristine and full of beauty because it gives us mental refuge from the toxic effects of society's constantly grinding gears. It's called

"Mother" Nature because we warm to the thoughts of its embrace upon us.

Nature can't be the villain, right?

Gary Giordano was admittedly wearing shoes. He complained they had felt heavy while swimming. In the surveillance video taken of him shortly after he alleges to have gotten out of the ocean and gone for help, he is positively seen wearing white sneakers. Robyn, it was reported, cut her foot on a rock. Obviously she had no footwear on at the time. So, it's safe to say that neither Robyn Gardner nor Gary Giordano wore fins during their swim.

From personal experience, I can attest to the fact that this is an extremely important consideration. I consider myself to be a capable and strong swimmer as well as a very experienced snorkeler. In addition, I exercise regularly and engage in an active lifestyle. While in the water, I have found myself in sudden and unexpected current shifts — ones that have required swimming with all my strength to escape. Once, less than a hundred yards from the beach in Maui, I looked up to realize an outgoing tide had pulled me out further than I had intended to go. As I swam hard for shore, there was a terrifying moment when I realized my fight was for naught — I wasn't making any headway and my arms were quickly getting exhausted. For the first time in my life, I got scared that I wasn't going to make it back and that there was a chance I was going to drown out there unless my fortunes changed quickly. I forced myself to kick even harder. After what felt like forever, I made it away from the current and into calmer water.

I wasn't wearing fins. It was a choice that could have resulted in disaster if I hadn't been confident in my abilities and my determination not to give up.

Fins add a considerable amount of propulsion to your kicks in order to power you through the water more easily and efficiently. The ocean is not like a steady pool. It is a constantly moving force that will push puny humans in whatever direction it chooses to take them. Currents are invisible forces with surprising and terrifying power. Snorkeling once off the island of Lanai, I was warned by the excursion boat crew not to venture past a certain point or I'd be quickly swept away in a current nicknamed "The Tahiti Express" — because that's where they would eventually end up finding my body thousands of miles away.

Considering that drowning is the third leading cause of unintentional injury death worldwide, claiming nearly 400,000 lives each year, it's hard to dismiss the possibility that Giordano, despite being of questionable character, was telling the truth about what happened out there.

Robyn and Gary Giordano had been drinking, both back at the hotel and at the Rum Reef Bar & Grill. If she was intoxicated and under the effects of a sleeping pill, she may have been overwhelmed by the situation, possibly disoriented.

Other possible scenarios include factoring the cut she received on her foot before going swimming in an area of the coastline known to have dangerous sharks.

If you are to believe the human trafficking angle, perhaps she was scooped out of the water by someone who sold her into the sex trade. Robyn was a blonde, just like the one desired by the 40 year old mystery man Joran van der Sloot alleges he met in a casino one night. Same height. Same weight. Almost identical.

Could Robyn have been spirited away to some human trafficking haven like nearby Venezuela — drugged and raped into submission, only to be sold to men in the Middle East, Asia or Africa for unspeakable purposes? Women in this life don't last long, often killed in inhumane ways when they become too old or "used up," their bodies disposed of in ways to ensure they will never be found.

Of course we would rather blame Gary Giordano. The alternatives are just far too horrifying to even contemplate. Take the bizarre case of David Potts, which I describe in "Fatal Sunset: Deadly Vacations." While vacationing on Maui in July of 2011, Potts visited a natural attraction known as the Nakalele Blowhole. A lava shelf that juts over the ocean, the blowhole is famous for geyser-like sprays launching up to a hundred feet into the sky when heavy surf crashes into the shore. Common sense dictates staying a safe distance from the hole, but Potts was dancing in the spray when a freak wave came up over the lava shelf and knocked him into the Nakalele Blowhole. In an instant, he was gone. Though police and Coast Guard searched for days, they never found David Potts' body.

April 23, 2012 marked what would have been Robyn Gardner's 36th birthday. Richard Forester spent the evening alone, giving a private toast to the girl he still loved. It had been months since there had been any communication from Aruba. Taco Stein has since left his post to become Solicitor General for the Windward Islands based on St. Maarten. Peter Blanken had been left in charge and was non-responsive.

"In Aruba, I think they are just happy it is off the island," said Forester.

To this day, Forester is still stung by accusations that the Robyn Gardner Foundation was his own private slush fund. "It is illegal to use funds for my own gain, it would land me in prison!" he declared.

However, Richard Forester is not so delicate when it comes to the subject of accuser Carla Baron.

"I will say that Carla Baron is a fraud with a failed career and any information she has provided is false," Forester told me directly. "I know I never hurt Robyn and I know what her last email(s) and Facebook messages to me said and they had nothing to do with breaking up with me...they were in fact the exact opposite of that. Carla Baron is a joke and she is only angry because I wouldn't allow her to be involved. All she wanted to do was attach her name to a high profile case in hopes of saving her career. She is a bottom feeder.

"I have nothing to defend. I know that, Robyn knows that and Robyn's family knows that. What the public thinks of me is of no concern. In fact, the only people that seem to have a problem with me are the very few people that buy into Carla Baron. I know I did the right thing for Robyn by stepping forward. I know I treated Robyn like a queen...as she deserved to be treated."

The oft-forgotten victims of vacation tragedy are those families, friends and loved ones left behind to mourn an inconsolable loss. They didn't ask for this; they deserve answers that, sadly, they will most likely never receive. All that hate has to go somewhere.

Less than two weeks before Christmas 2011, the following was posted on Facebook by the admins behind the "Help Find Robyn Colson-Gardner: Missing in Aruba" page.

"Gary....ARE YOU WATCHING THIS PAGE??? WHAT DID YOU DO WITH ROBYN? ANSWER ME ASSHOLE....I'M NOT GOING AWAY AND I WILL KEEP THE MEDIA PRESSURE ALL OVER YOU. YOUR AMBULANCE CHASING LAWYER DOESN'T SCARE ME AT ALL AND YOU ARE A SLIMEBALL COWARD. SPEAK UP! YOU LOOKED LIKE A LYING FOOL (EVEN MORE SO ON TV). WHY WOULD YOU INVOLVE YOUR KIDS? OH YEAH...BECAUSE YOU'RE A SLIMEBALL. SAY SOMETHING ASSHOLE. YOU KNOW HOW TO REACH ME. WHAT ABOUT YOUR FINANCES IN 2008, 2009, 2010 AND 2011? WHO CARES ABOUT 2005? THAT WAS 6/7 YEARS AGO ASSHOLE. WHY DID YOU SHOPLIFT? WHY DID YOU TRY TO SUE A

COMPANY FOR $5M AND THEN BACK OUT?....WE HEARD IT WAS BECAUSE DOCUMENTS WERE FORGED. YOU'LL NEVER GET AWAY FROM ME...I PROMISE YOU. WHERE IS SHE???????"

On Friday, August 16, 2012, *The Aruba Herald* posted the following story:

The first warning sign was placed at Baby Beach Thursday morning. Beach rules and warnings for certain areas are clearly stated on the sign. Locals as well as tourists have drowned at this beach in recent years because of the rip currents underflow, which takes them by surprise in certain areas in the ocean. Indications of dangerous areas will be placed in the water as well.

On the sign in clear to see red letters: *Life vests recommended.*

Vacation tragedies are most often complete flukes. Some come at the hands of predators. Others are due to being in the wrong place at the wrong time. Almost all of them share one thing in common: mistaking the initial absence of danger for absolute safety. It's an error in judgment that is easy to make and sometimes impossible to undo.

The truth is indeed ugly.

In August of 2005, shortly after the disappearance of Natalee Holloway, the still-interconnected human bones of a woman's forearm and hand were found washed up on Venezuela's Las Piedras Beach, on the southwest side of the Venezuelan peninsula, just 18 miles away from Aruba. Forensic tests performed were inconclusive.

Again, the spirited beauty stares back at me from the photograph. She's on a beach somewhere, relaxed and happy; my eyes keep dancing over her playful smile and those gleaming pearly whites. Her golden hair is barely restrained by a dark pair of sunglasses. A recently plucked orchid, the color of a ripe magenta mulberry, is tucked behind her ear. Her shoulders are tanned and toned, a marked contrast to the visible string of her black bikini top.

Time and again my gaze returns to her effusive smile, as large as life. Larger.

Her smile is alive. Her eyes are alive.

The smiling face that looks back at me from this photo wants to tell me something.

The smile is not born of abandon or whimsy, caught with the subject candid and unaware. No, this smile is intended for the camera, posed, a deliberate memory registered through the lens.

There's no doubt the smile is genuine. It's not worn like a mask to hide pain; there is nothing forced about it.

It is a happy smile, honest and intentional.

It is the grin of someone who, for this sliver of captured time, feels carefree and liberated from the burdens of life. It's a vacation smile.

It belongs to Robyn Colson Gardner and I can't stop staring at it. Her face utterly haunts me.

I just want to tell her something — the one thing I try to tell everyone.

Dare to be aware.

◊◊◊◊◊

The following is from the first Fatal Sunset book, "Deadly Vacations." Because of the connection between Aruba and the very suspicious disappearance of Amy Lynn Bradley, I felt it was worth mentioning.

AN EXCERPT FROM THE CHAPTER "CRUISE SHIP DISAPPEARANCES" FROM "FATAL SUNSET: DEADLY VACATIONS"

On March 24, 1998, twenty-three year old Amy Lynn Bradley also disappeared without a trace while traveling aboard the Royal Caribbean ship, *Rhapsody of the Seas* with her mother, father and brother.

Amy was a pretty, recent college graduate who attracted the attention of several crewmembers aboard the ship. According to her mother, "The waiters were very over-attentive towards Amy from the moment they met her. After dinner one evening, one of the waiters approached us while we were visiting with associates with whom we had been traveling and asked for Amy by name. The waiter stated 'they' wanted to take Amy to Carlos and Charlie's while docked in Aruba."

This was an invitation Amy chose to not only pass on, but also to not even acknowledge. "I would never do anything with any of those crewmembers. They give me the creeps," Amy responded. Instead, she and her brother chose to stay aboard the *Rhapsody of the Seas* instead of exploring Aruba.

"That same evening, March 23 (Monday), while docked in Aruba," added Amy's Mother, "all four of us attended a party on the upper deck, where the band was playing. We noticed a group of individuals standing alongside the railing who had boarded the ship with a dance troupe and who also were not passengers. They were not a part of the cruise! I wondered, how they could be allowed to board a ship and just stand around watching the performance with paying passengers? Looking back now, it seems even more dangerous to us."

Shortly afterwards, the Bradleys noticed something quite curious, and now-seemingly ominous. During the party, Amy and her mother ventured to the ship's fourth deck to check out photos that had been taken after dinner by the ship's photographer. To their surprise, every single one of Amy's photos was missing. Though the photographer claimed he remembered placing them out in the gallery where all of the other passenger photos were on display, the pictures had vanished.

The following day, during the early morning hours, Amy Lynn Bradley left her cabin with only her cigarettes and a lighter and was never seen again.

According to her mother, there was no way Amy had intended to be gone for long given that she hadn't even been wearing her shoes.

When Amy's parents couldn't locate her, they begged the ship's purser to search the ship and make an announcement. Also they requested Amy's photo be shown around to guests to ask if anyone had seen her. By lunchtime, the ship's captain told the Bradleys that he would not make an announcement that Amy was missing or post a picture for passengers to view for fear of "disturbing the guests." He assured the Bradleys that every inch of the ship had been searched.

The following day, with Amy still missing, Amy's parents left the ship to contact authorities. That day, they were informed by the F.B.I. that the only sections of the ship that had been checked were the common areas and restrooms.

On Thursday, March 26, Amy's mother, father and brother flew from Curacao to St. Maarten where they re-boarded the *Rhapsody of the Seas* and demanded a meeting with both the ship's captain and chief of security. Instead, they were greeted by a member of Royal Caribbean's 'risk management' team, who they later learned was an attorney assigned to represent the cruise line's interests against the Bradley family.

To date, according to Amy's mother, Royal Caribbean has failed to cooperate with the Bradley family in their search for answers to Amy's disappearance aboard their ship.

*****

FATAL SUNSET: DEADLY VACATIONS
is available in paperback and also for Kindle, Nook, iBooks, Kobo and as an audiobook.

TOP 10 "DARE TO BE AWARE" TRAVEL TIPS
I LEARNED WRITING FATAL SUNSET

Tip 1: Never assume you have the same rights, protections and access to emergency services in other countries as you do in your own.

Tip 2: Take the time to check out any attractions your children may use before you leave them unsupervised.

Tip 3: Always let someone know where you're going and how long you'll be gone. If you're on a trip, make sure someone in your party knows when you'll be back and check in with them if those plans change.

Tip 4: Don't assume that video cameras are there to protect you - They are only there to protect the interests of the property owners who may have a different agenda when it comes to revealing what those cameras have seen.

Tip 5: Just because there isn't a warning sign, doesn't mean there isn't danger - Use your common sense and/or double check your plans with someone who knows the lay of the land.

Tip 6: Do your research - Any reputable company offering trips, excursions, tours will have a digital footprint on the Internet. Use Google to search for reviews before you use them.

Tip 7: Be suspicious of anyone who takes too much interest in you or your family - If someone you really don't know invites you to join them in an excursion somewhere, don't be afraid to turn them down. There are worse things than offending someone who you will probably never see again.

Tip 8: If going out of the country, check for government issued travel advisories for your destination. If the state department says someplace is unsafe, take heed.

Tip 9: Being on vacation doesn't turn you into Superman - Don't try doing anything that may be more physically involved than something you would do at home.

Tip 10: Always listen and be kind to your flight attendant - He or she has much more experience than you in dealing with onboard emergencies and situations. Their help could save your life!

*****

ACKNOWLEDGEMENTS

First of all, my eternal gratitude to those of you who helped me discover the facts, because the truth is what we all want, right?

Special thanks goes out to: R. Lee Brown for being a really great editor.

And of course, as always, a big, big thanks to those of you who continue to buy, recommend and support my books!

BOOKS BY MARK YOSHIMOTO NEMCOFF

NON-FICTION:
- Tearing Down The Wall: The Contemporary Guide to Decoding Pink Floyd - The Wall One Brick at a Time
- Fatal Sunset: Deadly Vacations
- Where's My F*cking Latte? (And Other Stories About Being an Assistant in Hollywood)
- The Killing of Osama Bin Laden: How the Mission to Hunt Down a Terrorist Mastermind was Accomplished
- Go Forth and Kick Some Ass (Be the Hero of Your Own Life Story)
- Pacific Coast Hellway Presents - Pissed Off: Is Better Than Being Pissed On
- Admit You Hate Yourself
- Pacific Coast Hellway Presents - Porn vs. Chicken

FICTION:
- INFINITY (The Complete Saga)
- Transistor Rodeo
- Diary of a Madman
- Number One with a Bullet
- The Doomsday Club
- The Art of Surfacing
- Shadow Falls: Badlands
- Shadow Falls: Angel of Death
- Killing My Boss

ABOUT THE AUTHOR

Mark Yoshimoto Nemcoff is a bestselling and award-winning author who has been known to occasionally moonlight as a voice-over artist and independent journalist. He is a former Sirius Satellite Radio drive time show and T.V. host that has been featured by Playboy Magazine and Access Hollywood. He is the writer behind Kindle bestsellers "The Death of Osama Bin Laden" and "Where's My F***ing Latte?", an insiders look at the world of Hollywood celebrity assistants that was not only featured on Access Hollywood, but has spent over five years straight on Amazon's top-selling charts in the categories of "Television" and "Movies."

Mark currently resides in Los Angeles.

He can be reached at: MYN@WordSushi.com
Twitter.com/MYN
Facebook.com/MYNBooks

If you enjoyed this book, please tell your friends.
                                                    -MYN